Toward the Improvement

of Library Education

Toward the Improvement

of

Library Education

edited by

Martha Boaz

1973

Libraries Unlimited, Inc., Littleton, Colo.

TABLE OF CONTENTS

v

PREFACE

The position papers in this volume were written with the overall general objective of the "improvement" of library education. The immediate goal was to help establish a framework for future planning and for the improvement of professional education in library and information science. The project was carried out by Martha Boaz, as Senior Scholar in Residence, under the auspices of the United States Office of Education, through a grant to the Center for the Advanced Study of Technology, at the United States International University, San Diego, California.

The authors of the commissioned papers are leading librarians and library educators. One of the topics deals with general educational and social trends and their implications for library education. In other papers four types of library work are discussed under the main heading of "Library Education for the Future." These four papers deal with the public library, the special library, the university library, and the school library. Each of these papers tries to foresee the types of libraries and the library and information services which will be needed in the future. In addition, they try to outline plans for changing and improving library education so that librarians will be prepared to execute the duties, responsibilities, and skills which will be needed in libraries of the future. One rather specialized field is covered in the topic "Information Science: Its Place in the Library School Curriculum." In other papers questions are raised regarding library school curricula, and suggestions are given about ways and means to revitalize and improve professional education in library and information science.

After the commissioned papers had been prepared, a critic was asked to review each paper. On February 15-16, 1973, a two-day conference was held in Los Angeles, at the University of Southern California, for the purpose of reviewing, criticizing and discussing the papers. On the second day, the group divided into three small work groups to pursue the topics further and then reassembled to make recommendations about follow-up procedures. The last paper in this volume attempts to summarize the major points from the papers and from the conference discussion.

The participants in the group included the authors of the papers (with the

vii

exception of two who were unable to attend) and the critics of the papers. In addition, Dr. Stephen Abrahamson, of the University of Southern California School of Medicine, attended the session of the first morning and discussed some of the principles observed by other professions in revising their curricula. Miss Katherine Laich also attended the conference; she was there in two capacities—as president of the American Library Association and as a representative of the USC Library School faculty. She took notes and made a summary of the discussion; this summary was later forwarded to each person who attended the conference.

It is hoped that many of the recommendations can be implemented instead of being filed away under a Sears subject heading. It is suggested that local, regional, and national meetings might be held to consider ways to bring about change and improvement in library education.

Martha Boaz

PART I

ON SOCIAL CHANGE

LIBRARY EDUCATION: CHANGE IT, IMPROVE IT

Martha Boaz

Dean
School of Library Science
University of Southern California

The major concern of this paper is the improvement of library education and the establishment of a context for future planning. There are certain logical steps in such a futuristic study. These involve: trying to anticipate what the society of the future will be like; trying to determine what the library and information needs of this society will be; and trying to plan the type of library school education which will best prepare future librarians to give the information services which that society will need and require. An important step in this process should be an assessment of the information needs of users and non-users of libraries. What do people want and expect of libraries? What are their information needs? What will these be 30 years from now? How can their needs be supplied? After we know what types of libraries will be required, we can then determine the kind of education and training librarians will need in order to work in the libraries and information centers of the future. This assessment, however, is beyond the scope of this study and will not be discussed herein.

The paper will attempt to look ahead to the next 25 years, providing, and giving as background, a brief overview of the role of the library in society and some of the future social and cultural trends. This will be followed by a discussion of some of the general educational trends and some of the library education trends. Prior to these topics is a brief discussion of change and the need for planning for change.

Change and the Need for Planning It

People and institutions resist change; change is painful and slow. The intense desire for a new way of life is deeply rooted, however, especially within the younger generation, and change *will* take place.

The sixties were violent and revolutionary years. They were years of dialogue and confrontation, of concern with social and moral issues and with participatory democracy. The sixties were filled with multimedia, pop art, electronic and rock music, public television, and experimental video. Revolutions and violence were prevalent on university campuses. Students demanded a voice in the decision-making processes of their institutions. Academicians, administrators, and the nation learned that there are no easy answers.

The sad sixties and the sobering seventies have brought about a decline in the status of formal education. Education has its place and its function, but it cannot be all things to all men all of the time. Miracles may happen, but not often—and they seldom occur without human intervention.

The less dramatic seventies may be years of experimentation, trying new and different—perhaps radically different—ways of planning and problem-solving. The hard lessons learned in the sixties will be used to plan more sound and innovative programs for the future.

Change and Prophecy of Change

People, on the whole, do not anticipate great changes. They more or less assume that nothing will change very much, very soon. And, of course, change is not always progress. Many aspects of the future are beyond our control because there are so many unknown factors; but it stands to reason that we can determine at least the direction of some of these factors, for surely the future is too important to be left entirely to chance. Universal concern is being expressed about preparing for the future. The theory is to plan for change, not to let change overtake us.

"Our goal should be," says Simon Ramo of the Thompson Ramo Wooldridge Corporation, "that the future should happen not to us but because of us."[1] Ramo advocates more planning and studying of trends and future possibilities. He says, "We know we can't predict the future. But what will happen in the future is a possible foreseeable consequence of what we do now. Some future events are either too complex or will involve completely new discoveries that we couldn't have conceivably foreseen."[2] But, Ramo continues, "That we can't really predict the future is not an excuse for failure to anticipate certain things that could well happen. Our goal should be that what happens in the future should happen more or less because of us, not *to* us."[3]

The hope is that man *can shape his own destiny*, that the future will not be merely a matter of relentless destiny but of choice. One of the concerns of "futures" planners is not so much the direction of change but the rate at which change occurs and the impact this has on society.

Futuristics

Planning for a distant future has many pitfalls, and many policy makers who are also pragmatists generally are unwilling to take into consideration "blue sky" abstractions. But Charles W. Williams, Deputy Director of the Center for the Study of Social Policy, Stanford Research Institute, feels that "Many of our future options become feasible only if we are able to think in a framework of 20 or 40 years. Within that time period, it is conceivable to think about working out a complete transformation of our social system—a transformation that could give our society the qualities we would like for it to have."[4] Williams points out several possible views about change: 1) that the world of 30 years hence will be about as different from today's world as the world today is different from the world of 30 years ago; 2) that the rate of change has speeded up in recent years, so that the year 2002 would be as different from 1972 as 1972 is from 1892;

4

3) that the next 30 years will bring a change as enormous in scope as the industrial revolution; that is, the change during the next 30 years may be equal in scope to the change of the past two or three centuries! He said, "I believe this last view—though it utterly confounds our thinking—may be the most accurate."[5] As Williams pointed out, people may, in the future, accomplish in decades what previously required centuries.

One if the best-known advocates of the theory of adaptation of goals is Bertrand de Jouvenel, author of *The Art of Conjecture.*[6] He endorses a plurality of possible future plans and alternates, calling these "conjectured" future states "futuribles." His plan calls for decisions about what may seem the most desirable future state and for a course of action to carry out the plan. At the same time one assesses feedback and the possible consequences, then adjusts plans and goals and presents a range of alternate future states.

Since it is not possible to predict the future precisely, plans may very likely not indicate the best course of action, but they show the course that was considered best when the plan was developed. Error is to be expected, but change in plans should be a natural part of the process, after feedback and evaluation.

Alternate Futures

Intelligent planning will definitely create plans for alternate futures. Under this provision there can be a change of direction or the adoption of a course which may be more feasible as one gets closer to it than a course which had appeared more desirable at an earlier stage. Charles Williams says, "The articulation of alternate futures for entire nations and even for the world as a whole is . . . the greatest need of our time."[7] Williams points out that the future is shaped by human decisions and that "there now is a need for a 'new morality' in policy formulation: we must become conscious stewards of the future. . . ."[8]

In contrast to *prophecy*, which is distrusted, *planning* is considered to be a normative forecast and involves elements of choice. Planning is important in that it provides for decision-making. Otherwise, events may proceed to a point where only one choice can be made and no decision is allowed.

Because most of the changes that have taken place in American institutions of higher education have been responsive to changes in society, they should be examined against this background.

The individual of the future will need a new kind of education. He will have to plan his life to accommodate his own pace and to adapt to new social and organizational forms that will come into existence. The importance of this concept lies in this simple statement: needs determine values and values determine goals.

It behooves most of us to be interested in change and in planning for change, for, if we continue to live, the future will happen to all of us. Charles Kettering, an American inventor, said it this way: "My interest is in the future, because I'm going to spend the rest of my life there."

The Social Role of the Library

As an agency dealing with knowledge and the communication of information, the library plays an important and responsible role in the society of today.

The dependence on secondary and graphic records will increase as society becomes more complex. Nobody can deny that the world needs to collect more knowledge, and needs to communicate that which it already has. It can be concluded that the library is a logical agent to assist with the former and to carry out the latter. The need for information and for collecting it becomes more necessary as society becomes more complex. Information is important and new levels of awareness are mandatory for citizens in the creation of good public and social policies.

Knowledge in itself is valuable but the transmittal and use of knowledge are also of great value and justify the effort which so often goes into its discovery. Peter Drucker emphasizes this point when he says, "Only when a man applies information to doing something does it become knowledge. Knowledge, like electricity or money, is a form of energy that exists only when doing work."[9]

The library in its various settings plays various roles, according to the demands of its users: personal, group, or institutional. The traditional objectives of the library, particularly the public library, have been and are 1) the preservation of graphic records, 2) education 3) recreation and aesthetic appreciation, 4) personal enrichment and enlightenment, and 5) research. These objectives are important and will continue to be, but they imply a passive role for the library. Its future role will, without doubt, be actively involved with the dissemination of information, and with the maximum use of this knowledge and information. In the past we have waited for people to come to the library; in the future we must take the library to the people.

Information is of such value and is potentially so influential in what society does that it is very important for decision-makers in education, government, and industry to have access to the latest and most authoritative information. It is important that guidelines be found that will provide direction for the development of libraries, information centers, and library education.

Future Social Trends and Changing Values in Society

A new reformation is taking place in the re-thinking of traditional and current values. Without doubt these forces and values will affect libraries and library education, and they must be taken into account in the future planning of the entire library profession. The information which follows relates to future social trends and was obtained by use of the Delphi technique, developed by researchers at the RAND Corporation. The theory is that objective methods for exploring the future may come up with valid conclusions. Delphi is based on the simple premise that in making a forecast "X" number of heads are better than one. The technique is to use a set of procedures for forming a group judgment on speculative subjects. The usual procedure is to ask a group of 20 to 60 experts to make a forecast, anonymously, in response to specific questions. The questions are usually presented in large batches, in order to force experts to think about both near- and far-term events at the same time. The key to the technique is that all the panelists remain anonymous throughout the polling, which is usually done through the mail.

The author used the Delphi technique, including the following steps. A questionnaire was sent to a panel of experts knowledgeable in the areas. These

6

people were asked to try to forecast likely trends in particular fields. After the first questionnaire was received and the results tabulated, a second questionnaire was sent to the same panel indicating the median of each answer as tabulated from the first questionnaire. In this second interrogation the experts were asked to support their original answers or to change them if they preferred. Responses of the second questionnaire were tabulated and a summary prepared. Thus, something of a consensus was formed, the results of which are presented in the following pages.

Some of the Values and Trends

Research and development, the growth of technology, and certain social forces have caused great changes in society. Changes are also taking place in values and beliefs. Some of the predicted trends that may occur within the next 20 to 30 years and that may affect education as noted by the respondents to the Delphi questionnaire are:

1) There will probably be a significant decrease in the Puritan work ethic and a significant increase in leisure as a valid activity in its own right, with emphasis on pleasure, recreation, aesthetics, and self-fulfillment.

2) There will be a significant increase in involvement in social causes and in decision-making.

3) There will be continued and increased concern about ecology.

Opinions about the future probability of certain events indicated that we are highly likely to have continuing and increasing worldwide industrialization, new automation and advanced technology and, with the new technology, probably unemployment in certain fields; this unemployment will require frequent retraining programs for employees. It is quite likely that there will be continuing and increasing urbanization and megalopolitanization as well as an increased standard of living. Much of the present employment in general industry will shift to service industries. It is highly likely that there will be more minority race representation and more women in the work force in proportion to the population.

Because of improved nutrition and health care it is highly likely that people will live longer; one forecaster says many people may live to be 100 years old. It is desirable and quite likely that the average work week will be 35 hours or less and that vacations will be longer.

It is quite likely but very undesirable that there will be less privacy of information and an increase in the use of devices that encroach on the rights of the individual, such as wire-tapping and bugging.

Probability and Desirability of Certain General Educational Trends

Persons responding to the Delphi questionnaire checked probability and desirability of certain educational trends that may occur within the next 20 to 25 years:

1) Although very desirable it is unlikely that the institution of the community university will improve community life and provide cultural enrichment for the aged and unemployed.

2) It is desirable and as likely as not to happen that the public school will become a community center rather than remain a separate institution. And it is

7

desirable and quite likely that changes in the educational system will not originate entirely within the schools but will involve lay leaders and politicians.

3) Education will, as likely as not, take the lion's share of state and local finances, and it is both likely and desirable that higher education will become more involved in urban problems; it is also quite likely, yet very undesirable, that funding agencies may take over control of education.

4) It is as likely as not and desirable, according to the respondents, that schools will change from closed, controlled teaching institutions to innovative, experimental open learning and student-centered systems.

5) It is both likely and desirable that multi-campus programs and consortiums of institutions will increase and that educational programs for the culturally deprived will proliferate.

6) It is desirable and as likely as not that there will be a proportional increase in the number of people going to college and it is very desirable and quite likely that there will be a demand for quality education.

7) It is desirable and quite likely that there will be extended formal pre-school and post-secondary education; social as well as technological trends in a fast-changing world will increasingly require life-long learning and unlearning. Affluent families will have increased access to information in their homes due to advances in technology.

According to the predictions of the panel of experts the roles of teachers and methods of teaching will change to a considerable extent.

1) It is both likely and desirable that the single-teacher classroom will change to differentiated staffing, team teaching, guest lectures, and other different patterns. And it is likely and very desirable that education will increasingly focus on "How to Learn" instead of teaching specific facts.

2) It is as likely as not and desirable that student/teacher relations will change from the teacher as authority to a senior facilitator working with a junior colleague who is a student. It is also likely and desirable for teachers, because of frequent changes in education, to intersperse work with frequent periods of retraining. It is also considered likely that teachers will unionize and go on strikes, much as labor unions now do, for improved salaries and other personal benefits. The panel thought this would be an undesirable trend.

3) It is both likely and desirable that flexible scheduling, life-long learning and individual pace will prevail.

4) It is likely and desirable that computer-assisted instruction will be in general use by educators, the use of home terminals for education will increase, and there will be more independent study to fit individual needs.

5) Regarded as unlikely and very undesirable by the panel was the use of chemicals, drugs, and symbiosis to improve the learning process.

The prognosticators think there will be changes in requirements and grading within the next 20 to 25 years.

1) It is likely and desirable that required attendance will be replaced by optional participation in colleges and universities. It is likely and very desirable to have more exchange of credits from one school to another.

2) It is as likely as not that grades and degrees will tend to disappear and evaluation of students will be done by independent testing agencies; it is likely that institutions other than schools will serve as credentialing agencies. All of

these possibilities are considered to be undesirable by the respondents.

3) It is likely as not and desirable that internationally owned communications satellites will be used for mass education.

4) It is also quite likely and desirable that data be assembled on the use of new technologies and on the extent of innovation practiced.

Research and its importance have been discussed at length for many years. The panel of experts thinks it quite likely and desirable that there be increased emphasis on research and on obtaining data about the needs of learners, how they learn, when and where they learn. It is as likely as not and desirable that higher education will have an increased role in policy research and will make it available to top policy makers in government.

Developments in Libraries and Information Centers
That Should be Considered in Library Education

Certain developments and trends are noticeable in the fields of libraries, librarianship, and information science. The panel of experts indicated agreement or lack of it and gave opinions, also, about the desirability or undesirability of the developemnts.

The panel agreed with and considered desirable the following trends. The library will become a center for many activities not traditionally associated with it. Information centers and libraries will become influential change agents, and librarians will become more involved in assisting with the solution of community problems; it is quite likely and desirable that there will be more library involvement with other community and government agencies such as business, industry, labor, social organizations, museums and other agencies. There will be more cooperative information networks; these will serve homes as well as libraries; a global library-information network system will be inevitable in the future. Libraries will make greater use of publicity and public relations techniques.

It is considered agreeable and desirable, also, that libraries will be working more with media in behavioral and communication fields and that the computer will be as omnipresent in the future, in independent institutions and homes, as is the telephone today. A universal computer language and a universal cataloging and classification system for library materials are quire likely and very desirable. The use of public cable television channels for educational purposes will be in general use in 10 years, and libraries of the future may have responsibility for production as well as distribution of education and communication materials.

Developments in Library Education

The experts were asked to respond to certain aspects of library education. On the following points they agreed *strongly* and considered to be *very desirable* that:

1) Library education programs should be more innovative.

2) More educational options should be open to both instructor and student.

3) Library school curricula should be designed to prepare students to anticipate developments, solve problems, and adapt to change.

4) Library school graduates of the future should have more knowledge of automation.

On several other points the feeling was not as strong but the terms "I agree" and "Desirable" were used for the following:

1) Librarians will need more training for involvement in community affairs and services.

2) Library school students should take more responsibility for their own self-development.

3) Library schools should take the lead in initiating change in libraries.

4) There should be more on-the-job training (field work) in the library school curriculum.

5) Library education as it is today will be obsolete in 20 years.

The panelists disagreed and considered very undesirable that library education should continue more or less as it is presently structured. They were neutral as to whether or not library education should merge with a cluster of other professional and specialized disciplines and about whether there should be more specialists from other professions such as business, engineering, psychology, and communications.

They disagreed that library technicians should do most of the work now being done by librarians, but they thought it likely and very desirable that more use be made of paraprofessionals in libraries.

They agreed and thought it desirable that the school librarian have knowledge of how people learn and be thoroughly familiar with new curricular developments; that the special librarian have specialized subject knowledge; that the public librarian should have knowledge of community and political structure and social problems; that the college and university librarian have a liberal arts background as well as special subject knowledge.

They thought it likely and desirable that there would be more need for more subject specialists, for more librarians with information science knowledge, for more with research backgrounds, and for more library school graduates holding doctoral degrees in fields other than library science.

Other Reports

Findings of the Delphi questionnaire are borne out by a number of other reports. The following material extends and adds to the Delphi findings. Reports of the United States Bureau of Labor Statistics[10] and the Bureau of the Census[11] give trends and predictions about the population, the economy, employment and other items that educators and librarians must take into account in any realistic planning.

Population and Labor Force 1980

Libraries and library schools will be affected by the size of the population, which is expected to rise to 322 million by the year 2000. It is predicted that the labor force, by 1980, will climb by one-fifth to 100 million workers, that the educational level of the labor force will have risen substantially, and that it will include a large number of young workers (26 million) between the ages of 25 and 34. In the 45 to 64 age group the figure will be barely 5 percent higher than now; older people will probably retire earlier as there will be better retirement income for all and opportunities for older people, with better health and longer life expectancy, to pursue new avocations or interests, or continued education. Women workers have increased, with 40 percent of all the women in the country now being in the labor force. In 1950 only 28 percent of the women worked. Women headed one-tenth of all families in 1970. It is expected that the number of women workers will continue to increase as more day-care centers for children are established.

By 1980, according to predictions, the number of black workers will increase by one-third. One-sixth of the 1970 population was either foreign-born or born of foreign or mixed parentage. About 15 percent, or 30 million Americans, told the census-takers that the English language was not their mother tongue. More than one out of every seven workers in 1970 worked for a federal, state, or local government agency.

One of the interesting findings in the 1970 census study was the dramatic change in industry employment and the shift toward service-producing industries. Early in this century only three in every ten workers were in service industries. In 1980 close to seven in every ten workers, or 68 million, are projected to be in service industries. The Census Bureau's statistics certify that the United States now has a white-collar economy; this category extends from professional to clerical work. The trend will continue, with blue-collar jobs diminishing and white-collar occupations increasing; the latter will require education and training beyond that needed by blue-collar workers. Within the labor market, unions will emphasize take-home pay instead of job security.

Hours of work will decline slightly during the 1970s at 1 percent a year. In the more distant future there will probably be a 30-hour work week and a three-day weekend; as a consequence of the shorter work week, people will have more time for personal development and self-fulfillment.

The Shape of U.S. Economy 1980

By 1980, Gross National Product (GNP), growing at a rate of 4.3 percent each year, will have reached $1.4-trillion in 1968 dollars. The projected GNP for 1980 will be 65 percent above the level of 1968. In 1970 one-fifth of all U.S. families had incomes of over $15,000 a year; the median family income was $9.590—an increase of 70 percent over 1960's $5,660.

By 1980 consumers are expected to spend close to $900-billion on goods and services, and governments are expected to be spending more on domestic problems, with the state and local governments' shares of the GNP rising from 11.6 percent in 1968 to 12.8 percent in the services economy in 1980. The lion's share of funds at state and local levels will go to education.

A great deal of government money will be spent on public health, hospitals, and sanitation. National concern for health care will lead to regional and community health centers, hospitals, nursing homes, and establishments for the aged and the mentally and physically handicapped. There will be *free*, perhaps even *compulsory*, health care as there is now free public education.

Basic assumptions underlying the economic prognostications are: 1) the institutional framework of the American economy will not change radically; 2) although the international climate will change (for the United States will not be involved in a major war), a still guarded relationship will not allow a major reduction in arms.

11

Education and Manpower

"Education is today the major occupation of 63.7 million people in the United States,"[12] says W. Vance Grant. He continues, "That figure, along with the fact that more than $90-billion will be spent by educational institutions this year, lends credence to the contention that education is now the nation's largest enterprise . . . more than three out of every ten persons are directly involved in the educational process."[13] S. P. Marland, Jr., the U.S. Commissioner of Education, points out that "the goal is quality education for all . . . [but] we will never achieve all we want from education if for no other reason than that what we want is constantly being redefined in terms of new career requirements and higher personal expectations. Thus there will be an enduring discontent, a constant demand for renewal."[14]

Education and Educated Manpower

High enrollments in colleges and universities will continue in spite of a slowdown in population growth; the reason for this is that a larger proportion of the population will be attending college. The median number of school years completed by Americans over 24 years old was 12.1 in 1970, compared with the 10.6 in the 1960s. By 1980 the number of Bachelor's degrees will climb by two-thirds and Master's and Doctor's degrees will double by 1980.

Marked changes will take place in schools. Some forward-looking teachers are predicting that 50-minute class periods will be only a memory in another 20 years, that teachers will become directors of computer-based learning systems, that children do not necessarily learn best in a traditional classroom. The overall theory is that education is something a teacher does to a student.

With increasing automation and with the rapid advances in knowledge will come the need for people with highly specialized knowledge. But—these specialities will soon become obsolete and will increase the need for adult and continuing education through a lifetime. Few people will say, as they did in the past, "When I finished my education." It will be possible and quite likely that one individual will have two or three careers.

There may be amazing advances in behavior control through chemical and electronic means and a doubling of intellectual capacity through chemical, electronic, or surgical methods. All of these ideas have implications for education, learning, and libraries.

Trends in Elementary School Education

Certain schools are experimenting with performance contracting on the elementary school level. The Los Angeles Board of Education in July 1972 took its first cautious step in this area.[15] The Board expressed its intent to seek state funds to hire a private company to train teachers in mathematics and reading instruction, the company to be paid on the basis of how well students succeed. In Los Angeles the teachers in the city schools would still conduct all classroom instruction, contrary to some performance contracts, in which the private company has charge of the whole program.

The success of this experiment is debatable. Teacher organizations have generally opposed it, whereas private companies have claimed success for the technique. Pupil progress is measured by a series of tests given before, during, and after the program. The tests must be approved by the state.

Elementary Education

In California two landmark school reforms were approved by the State Board of Education in April 1972; these called for the opening of classrooms to four-year-olds and equalized financing of public education under a statewide property tax.[16] The schooling for four-year-olds is an effort to reach children when they are receptive and less inclined toward apathy. These would both require approval of the Legislature and the Governor. The shift of school property taxes from local districts to the state and the spending of large additional money on low-income students are significant trends in public education.

The plan of State Superintendent Wilson C. Riles would radically change public schooling for children up to the age of eight. New kinds of schools similar to community centers would be created. Here all educational, social, medical, and other public services are combined into a comprehensive program under the direction of teachers, parents, specialists, and youth volunteers. Local districts would be free to develop their own early childhood programs, but the state would exercise strong control under a master plan drawn up by the State Board. The Board and the State Department of Education would monitor and evaluate local programs and use of state funds would hinge on acceptable progress of students as determined by achievement test scores. The term "community school" is also used to describe facilities that would function every day as centers for all age groups in all neighborhoods under wholly local control.

Americans are Restless

Census Bureau figures suggest that Americans are a restless people. In 1970, one-fourth of all Americans were living in a different state from the one in which they were born. The 1970 census shows that 20 percent of the population changes residence annually, but the pattern of settlement is becoming distorted. Concentration of population is directed to coastal areas and westward. The question may be, population analysts say, not how to accommodate new population, but how to arrange the population we already have. A conscious plan for rearrangement, encouraging future growth away from the large urban regions into smaller communities, seems feasible. The mobility of almost all citizens has implications for students who no longer go to a single school system throughout their educational studies and who must be taught to adapt to learning and job requirements in different places.

Changes in the Library World

Many people in the library profession do not agree that change is needed in the library world, in libraries themselves, or in library education. They continue to think of the library as a collection of books and as a place to which people come for reading materials or for quick answers to reference questions.

What is the role of the library? What is its responsibility? What services should be provided by library and information centers? Does the library survive as an institution for the sake of institutionalism or does it exist to serve its clients and their needs? The library profession must decide what its role is to be.

Is the library a passive traditional organization or an active agency concerned with extending knowledge, going out to people, providing them with assistance which will enable them to know more and be better informed to help them solve problems and to contribute to the advancement of society?

Increasingly important in contemporary thinking is the theory that librarians should go out to the people, sell their wares, make libraries indispensable; in this way will they be supported, maintained, improved, and extended. In line with business theory, it is recommended that libraries should work as though they were in business—and in business to make money—as though their very existence depended on whether or not they sold their products, as though giving more and better service to more and more people would ensure a posterity for libraries. For this is so. Otherwise, financial support for libraries will decrease, services will diminish, collections will become dead warehouses, and inventory centers and information services will be taken over by some other more active, energetic, and intelligent group or agency. The clarion call goes out: ACTION is needed! Action is needed NOW if the library profession is to survive in any important or distinctive professional capacity.

Libraries and Library Education

The decline of the prestige of educational institutions has led to a realization of the potentials and possibilities of self-education, and it is here that the library "comes into its own." But it will have to change if it is to go far in a competitive world. As Ellsworth Mason has put it, "If Muhammed won't come to the library, we must bring the library to Muhammed."[17] Mason says,

> We are going to have to do away with the idea of a great fixed-location central library . . . and think more of a central warehouse for collection, a storage and issuing point, and fluidly moving, constantly changing, much smaller branch libraries whose central function will be to get readers interested, and serve as substations for the central warehouse that will have become a pumping station.[18]

Mason comments on various trends and technological changes but says they will reemphasize the values to be found in the kinds of materials in libraries.

The librarianship of the future seems oriented to the social and behavioral sciences, but the library profession will undoubtedly retain its interest in the field of the humanities and should continue to give full service in the field.

Lowell Martin speaks of changes in libraries, the responses that librarians must make to them, and predicts changes:

> . . . from a people seeking productivity alone to a people also seeking value and fulfillment; from an educational system concerned with numbers to one seeking to develop quality; from a society of workers to a society of specialists; from a readership limited to the elite to a readership extended to the underprivileged; from the first step of building strong collections to the further step of outreach of resources through the whole society; from the traditional book to communica-

tion in new and ingenious forms; from routines that sap our time and energy to machines that free us; from your own separate library to a unit within an area-wide resource; most important, from an assumption that what we do is automatically socially significant to a professional recommitment to library purposes.[19]

These Changes in Libraries will Mandate Changes in Library Education

Neal Harlow has asked an important question: "Do we as educators have the insight and then the courage and strength to attempt to change the nature of the social institution called the library by changing the behavior of librarians?"[20] Harlow proposes "for the library school curricula at this time a great rending earthquake rather than a bit of adjustment along the old line."[21]

We can no longer wait to begin the change in library education until all circumstances are in the right orbit or until a perfect theoretical plan appears, for as Richard Bellman says, we must find some "sensible and scientific approach to human affairs, without awaiting the elaboration of impeccable theories. The complexity of human existence cannot be explained by one all-embracing theory. A number of local theories are required."[22]

In its planning process, library education should take a hard look at what other professionals are doing. At the same time in examining the purpose and significance of professional education attention should be given first to the purpose and meaning of education in general. The traditional concept of education has been to transmit to the emergent generation those parts of a society's culture which it considers fundamental for its own stability and survival. A second theory of education is that it trains leaders for the progress of the group by developing new ideas and preparing for adjustment to the changing environment. Thus, paraphrasing W. E. Hocking, the first function of education is *reproduction of the type* and then promoting *growth beyond the type*.

Jenks and Riesman hypothesize that "the function of a professional school is not primarily to teach a narrowly defined set of skills of the kind measured by examinations, but to define a set of general criteria that recruits to the profession ought to meet and to screen out those who do not measure up."[23] The authors point out that professionalism is on the rise rather than on the wane and that this is a basic trend that will shape higher education in the future.

The library profession must reexamine its role in society and then its concepts of both the general and professional requirements for admission to the field. W. E. Hocking's description of the two functions of education may apply equally to library education, for without doubt the library profession should probably reproduce some of its present type of education but should also grow beyond this type if it is to fulfill a necessary and expanded information-communication-transmission role in society.

Innovation is Needed

There has been much talk and a ferment of ideas about innovation in library education in recent years. Articles have been written, conferences have been held, and academic faculties have talked at length about curriculum changes and improved teaching methods; but the efforts have been sporadic and little has been done of an innovative nature. The need for change has not resulted in

15

change. The reasons may be a fear of departing from the known traditional patterns or it may simply be a matter of lethargy. But bold implementation and strong action are required if change is to take place.

It is unlikely that any innovation of consequence will take place in library education until there is pressure from the outside profession (the practitioners), from inside the library school (faculty and students), and, hopefully, from users of libraries. Such change and reformation will be based upon obviously perceived need on the part of the profession or it will come as the result of dynamic brilliant leadership in the profession.

Library education and library schools are often criticized by students and by practitioners. The criticism is frequently justified, for many library educators, like many library practitioners, are not aware that the changes taking place in society demand change in libraries and in library education. Paul Wasserman comments on the attitude of library educators: "Where there is sensitivity, it tends to relate only to suggestions of broadened book collections in order to cover all sides of an issue, or to focus upon technical matters devolving about fair representation in catalogs as they deal with people and ideologies."[24] Wasserman continues:

> When library educators do center their attention upon the field, it is invariably within the existing framework, rather than as detached observers perceiving it from outside. And when they participate in councils of librarianship, it is as fully as partisans of the existing structure as any in practice. The critical nature of scholarly questioning tends to be absent. The ends of professional effort are seldom in question. Thus does library education abdicate its responsibility for leadership.[25]

Tightening Admission to Get Better Alumni

One way to shape and strengthen the library profession is to tighten the admission and screening standards for admission to the profession. Jenks and Riesman have suggested that only those be admitted who, in the opinion of the educators, have the proper qualifications.[26] This can be done by setting intellectual qualifications; by enforcing age restrictions, and by providing special rewards to few students. Jenks and Riesman argue that:

> This sorting and certifying is considerably more important than what the schools actually try to teach. Just as it is easier to change the character of a college by changing the admissions requirements than by changing the curriculum, so too it is easier to change a profession by recruiting new sorts of apprentices than by changing the rules of the apprenticeship. Professional schools have their students for only a few years, and they can do only so much with whatever raw material they get. But to the extent that they are overapplied and can select their raw material according to some preconceived plan, they can influence the profession they serve decisively.[27]

Leaders are Needed

Leaders in institutions and in professions often set the standards for their organizations and professions. Leadership capabilities and charisma are necessary to plan, organize, and implement new programs and services in library education and in libraries. An educational foundation might, if convinced of the need, support 12 young people who could be educated and trained for leadership roles. Twelve brilliant, interested, and dedicated young leaders might revolutionize the profession.

The types of individuals who are needed are ones who have the intelligence, the ability, the enthusiasm, the energy, the magnetism, and the influence to change and redirect librarianship. This means more than changes in the technical aspects of computer technology and automation, which deal mainly with mechanical progress. It means a change in the concepts of the library profession's *raison d'être* for its leadership role in supplying the information needs of the people. The importance of information and its influence on world development in a complex period in history cannot be disputed. The library profession holds a great responsibility and an enormous privilege. And certainly the library profession needs leadership—young people with ideas and vision, enthusiasm and energy, drive and dedication. Until it can attract such leaders, it will be a pedestrian profession which may or may not survive as a profession. It may devolve to technician or paraprofessional status.

Our educational program—both general and professional—for the librarian should give him the knowledge, the background, and the intellectual discipline to guide him in the solution of problems and in the pursuit of a professional life which is personally satisfying and socially beneficial. The library profession, perhaps more than any other profession, is concerned with the integration of all branches of knowledge and with all spheres of activity in its services, hence the need for a broad general education in addition to subject specialization.

The librarian of today and of the future must be equipped to work in a social milieu in which heavy intellectual, social, and professional demands will be made on him. He will need a superior general and professional education and must be qualified and competent to work in an environment where a great variety of demands will prevail.

The librarian must have certain basic knowledge which relates to the role and objectives of the library; he must be interested in and informed about human knowledge and the records that contain this knowledge; he must be well founded in the theoretical background and current concepts of his field; he must be well informed in his field of specialization; he must be acquainted with and able to perform research in his own professional area; he should have some interdisciplinary experience which gives him an appreciation of the integration and interdependency of knowledge.

Systems Concept in Library School Curricula
The application of the systems concepts to higher education is a late development and the use of systems principles in the operation of libraries is in its infancy. These new thrusts have brought about new methodologies, techniques and tools for libraries and information systems. Systems analysis has a great potential for the development of integrative curricula and for new teaching resources, as well as for data gathering and research.

Argument for the "Systems" Approach

Decision-making, in the "systems" concept, involves interaction. This is especially important in complex issues which require the knowledge of various experts before the whole issue can be understood. Group effort is required in synthesizing the different pieces of a total program. Dr. Simon Ramo, Executive Vice-President of the Thompson Ramo Wooldridge Corporation, is a leading exponent of the "systems" approach. He uses this theory in the company with which he is associated as well as in many other corporations and professional associations that he directs and advises.

A Systems Approach to Curriculum Planning

Martha Jane Zachert has outlined a systems approach to planning a curriculum for special librarianship. She lists nine steps:[28] 1) establish the objectives of the curriculum; 2) identify the components of the library/information system; 3) define the human jobs; 4) specify the acceptable performance of each component of the human job; 5) reexamine the performance within the total environment; 6) consider the resources and restraints; 7) postulate the curriculum; 8) test the plan; 9) redesign.

Mrs. Zachert explains that step eight requires a test of the curriculum with actual students. Although the above list was applied to special librarianship, it seems equally valid for the general library school curriculum.

Need for Research

The library profession is young and has had little time to pursue or develop research of any consequence. But research is mandatory if librarianship is to have respect as a profession, and the profession should generate knowledge in the pure and theoretical disciplines. It is from these sources that the field will establish its intellectual foundations. Research is needed, also, in a very practical sense as a base for scientific planning; facts are necessary to obtain funding for the development of libraries and their services. Agnes Griffen and John Hall comment on the dearth of factual evidence that might assist in bringing about library change: "We do not now have any parameters that will enable us to evaluate the effectiveness of library services, much less changes for better or worse. Beyond intuition, all we have are a few library statistics and they are not standardized."[29]

Research and a climate conductive to research are necessary for experimentation in libraries and in library education. The profession must use scientific methods in studying its own problems. The profession should have a National Institute of Research, funded by a foundation or the government, which could give leadership and direction in the field. In addition, each school should have a research component or at least a faculty team with responsibility for conducting and directing research.

Research about learning, about how people learn, and about teaching is needed. What is good teaching, and what are the characteristics of a good teacher? Can such characteristics be developed? These are some of the questions; research is needed to find the answers.

The function and role of the library should be defined before setting up elaborate and costly future library programs. Also antecedent to planning specific programs there must be a set of clearly defined library objectives. These objectives will of necessity have to inculcate the philosophy of the library profession. Thus, a program of research should be instituted to determine how best to achieve the stated objectives, obtain the necessary funding to execute them, and put the program into action. Otherwise, librarianship operates in a vacuum and arrives nowhere with nothing.

General Basic Library School Program

The program of the library school should provide the student with: 1) an understanding of the role of the library as an educational and information agency; 2) a knowledge of the principles of administration and organization required to fulfill the objectives of the library (this includes personnel, physical facilities, collections and programs of service); 3) an understanding of the theories of collecting, building, and organizing library materials for use; 4) a considerable knowledge of the intellectual content of graphic records and an ability to assist the user of library materials in locating and interpreting desired items; 5) a specialization that is of particular interest as a career objective. This may be centered in the library school or it may involve interdisciplinary study in other divisions of the university; 6) a basic knowledge of the principles of research which will be used to advance the profession of librarianship.

After determining the educational goals and behavioral objective, the schools must select and organize educational experiences that will logically lead to goal achievement; the faculty arranges for students to have varied means for learning, and then faculty and students determine whether the goals have been attained.

The order of curriculum, the required and elective courses, should be based on a general plan for equipping a student with the knowledge, skills, and intellectual tools to serve as a professional person in a library which is fulfilling its role in society. The intellectual content and the concepts of the curriculum should be presented in a logical order. This is a sound principle of curriculum development, but it is not always followed in practice.

Newer Course Content

Within recent years, mainly due to advances in technology, new courses and techniques have been introduced into the library school curriculum. These are concerned more with physical form, method, and use than with content in the traditional sense of course content. The courses include these fields: audiovisual and microphotography (sometimes falling under the more comprehensive heading "instructional technology"); documentation, information retrieval, and information science. In the early years information retrieval was largely concerned with the use of computers for the storing and handling of information, but soon attention was given to the theory, philosophy, and foundations of information science, and it is now considered by many to be a complete discipline in itself. Information science is now commonly regarded as an accepted part of the librarian's education. It seems to be inevitable that library schools of the future will become more involved with this field. The two disciplines of librarianship and information science will become definitely

19

interfused, with both focusing on information—its organization, storage, retrieval—and dissemination for use.

Library Practice

In earlier years, many library schools required the student to have supervised practical library experience as a part of his degree program, but this requirement was dropped by most of the schools during the 1950s. A renewed interest in practice or work-study has developed within the last few years. This has evolved from students' requests that their educational courses be "relevant." Of course, says one critic of the so-called 'relevance,' "What is relevant today may be completely irrelevant tomorrow." Another educator has said, "A relevant course is a vocational course."

A carefully planned work-study or internship program, coordinated with classroom theory, is undoubtedly a valuable and meaningful experience for a student. This internship should, of course, be well supervised by persons who themselves are highly qualified professional people.

Use the City as an Educational Institution

Extended practice work might be useful in library school curricula. "If we can make our urban environment observable we will have created classrooms with endless windows on the world."[30] This provocative idea was the theme for the 22nd annual International Design Conference in Aspen, Colorado. Theories of education related to community design and alternative educational programs were proposed. These included suggestions about using theaters, normally empty by day, for classrooms with sophisticated audiovisual equipment built in. Colossal slide-film-videotape-soundtrack equipment is available from a number of sources.

A bus might be used as a mobile school house, as has been done at UCLA by architecture professor Charles Rusch. Means of getting out of the classroom and into the city should be planned, so that information agencies and educational processes can interact.

Students should probably be encouraged to take courses in alternative library schools. Library schools should think in terms of changing educational methods to make better use of the outside world as a learning place.

New Approach—No Grades, No Majors—Interdisciplinary Approach

There has been much discussion of the values of interdisciplinary study, and many library educators have been among those advocating this plan. One approach to interdisciplinary study is through an experimental unit within a traditional program. Evergreen State College at Olympia, Washington, has tried an interdisciplinary curriculum; it has abandoned departments and majors, grades, faculty committees, and faculty tenure. This program was begun by Charles J. McCann, former dean of the faculty at Central Washington State College. McCann's theory is that students should learn how to learn so they can adjust quickly to the rapid changes in modern life. He assembled a task force of 60 people to work out the business and academic details of the program before the first 1,100 students arrived on the campus in the fall of 1971. The most important part of the planning centered on the curriculum and focused on

20

interdisciplinary seminars. "Known as 'coordinated studies' programs, these seminars seek to combine the special knowledge of professors from several fields in the discussion and study of a single broad topic."[31] The size of the seminars varied from three faculty members and 60 students to six faculty members and 120 students, a low ratio by most standards. Some of the seminars last a quarter, some a year.

The student moves from the coordinated seminar to a program of "contracted studies." In this the student signs a contract with a faculty member listing what he wants to learn and within what time period. The student and the professor, working together, plan a contract giving the purpose and goals, the number of units to be earned, and the time limit. Thus, the student is involved in setting his own goals and in judging the results. During the period of the total program, the student must have some practical work experience. The Evergreen College student taking both "coordinated" and "contracted" studies accumulates 36 units of credit for graduation. This ordinarily would take four years but may be completed in three.

Grades are not used for Evergreen students. Instead, they assemble portfolios showing examples of their work and detailed evaluations by their professors. Faculty members also have portfolios which emphasize their teaching talents rather than research. Professors do not have tenure, but their work and their continued employment is reviewed every three years.

Curriculum

In planning a library school curriculum, some of the required and/or recommended courses might or might not be offered in the library school. Following the theory of interdisciplinary study, a student might take courses such as administration, budgeting, and management in a school of business administration, or an audiovisual course in a department of instructional technology or a course about library buildings in a school of architecture.

Departing from Traditional Curriculum

Efforts are being made in some academic areas to depart from required courses. In one library school, "competence may be acquired in a number of ways: through previous study or experience, through course work in the school, through course work in other departments, through internships, through work experience concurrent with formal study or through directed individual study. Formal credentials will be used to determine competencies (degrees, official transcripts of academic work, a thesis, publications, scores on tests and examinations, etc.). We feel this decision is a departure from the rigidity and formalism so characteristic of many programs. . . ."[32]

This flexible plan will emphasize individual goals and efforts and tested abilities rather than a specific number of courses and examinations. There are complications and problems to deal with before this program can be fully effective, but solutions can undoubtedly be worked out.

Teaching and Teaching Methods

The idea of recruitment of potential future leaders and careful screening of applicants for admission to library school is directed, on the whole, toward getting better practitioners in the profession. At the same time, consideration should be given to recruitment of better teachers in library schools. A good faculty in a school is its most important asset. Quality education can be had only if quality faculty provide it. Each course is largely a matter of the individual faculty member's expression and interpretation of it. The teacher's knowledge, background, education, experience, personality, and interest in the subject and the student are important factors. More important than any of these, perhaps, is enthusiasm. One of the limitations of library schools has been the lack of qualified superior teachers. Planning for the improvement in library education should definitely include the recruitment of excellent teachers. Inseparable from this is the provision for salaries that will attract and hold these teachers.

Good teachers are constantly seeking new methods and techniques for improving their instruction. They are experimenting with various physical devices such as television, filmstrips, records, recordings, and other modern new forms. Instead of emphasis on rote memory, good instructors help students learn to think, to attain knowledge about how to solve problems and to recognize the value of considering alternate solutions to problems.

Limitations of the One-Year Graduate Program

A one-year graduate education program presents a number of problems, including lack of depth and breadth in both the choice of classes and their content. These problems exist if the student takes all of his courses within the library school, and they are multiplied if he is in an interdisciplinary program. It is difficult to become well informed—much less, steeped in any profession— within a one-year period. A two-year curriculum is certainly more desirable, but many students cannot afford to spend either the time or the money on a two-year program.

Changing Values

Values are being questioned and changes are taking place in general education and in library education. In some library schools admission requirements are changing, grading systems are being challenged, comprehensive examinations are being dropped, the number of "required" courses is being lowered, work-study programs are being revived, individual study programs are being promoted and students are participating in decision-making processes once regarded as the responsibility of the faculty.

Student involvement and activism in the 1960s was accompanied by demands for student participation and involvement in the decision-making and administrative processes of educational institutions. This has been followed by the participation of students in many of the activities formerly engaged in by more mature and experienced faculty and administrative personnel. There are mixed reactions to this development. It is generally agreed that students should participate in affairs that concern them, but in many instances they have voiced complaints without providing solutions and in some cases with chaos instead of progress as a result.

Importance of Contact with Library Practitioners

Contact with practitioners in the field is important for the library school. The library school, generally considered the "whipping boy" of the profession, often has guilt pangs about its own incompetence. Jenks and Riesman give a contrary opinion: "At any given moment the quality of practice taught at a professional school is likely to be higher than that actually carried on by the alumni of the school."[33] Some schools have an advisory council composed of representatives from various types of libraries. Members of the council give advice and suggestions to the school about curriculum content and continuing education needs. They sometimes ask the school for help in solving certain of their problems. "Practicing librarians" are often invited to give lectures to students in either classroom or colloquium settings. The goal of this contact and exchange of ideas between the schools and the practitioners is that both will be assisted in the advancement of the profession.

Social Action

Interest in social action is not new in librarianship. Library leaders from the time of the early 1930s have been vigorous in their fight to make the library, especially the public library, a dynamic social institution with an important mission, role, and responsibility in improving man's condition and society's progress. Librarians are becoming increasingly involved in the defense of intellectual freedom, and in social action outreach programs in communities. These programs usually involve working with other community agencies. It has been suggested that the public library would be a suitable agency for coordinating and mobilizing total information resources of the community.

Certainly these changes in society will mandate changes in library and information services and in the curricula of library schools. And library education should initiate change, not merely react to it; it should lead in innovation, not follow practice. It should be active, not passive, in its role within the library profession.

Pilot Experimental Programs

Curriculum revision and adoption of change is difficult to bring about by consensus or on a national scale. In all likelihood one or two institutions will lead the way by experimentation, and by trial and error. Without doubt there will be failures, but only by trying will change be brought about and progress made. It is to be hoped that one or several schools will volunteer to be prototypes and to set up pilot experimental programs designed to supply the future information needs of society; that plans will be made for several alternate methods to reach the curriculum goals; and that the curricula of these schools will train librarians and information specialists to follow the example of medicine in its concern for every patient and for the well-being of society as a whole.

FOOTNOTES

[1] Digby Diehl, "Q and A: Simon Ramo," *Los Angeles Times, West Magazine*, May 21, 1972, p. 23.

[2] *Ibid.*

[3] *Ibid.*

[4] Charles W. Williams, Jr., "Inventing a Future Civilization," *The Futurist*, VI (August 1972), 137-38.

[5] *Ibid.*, p. 138.

[6] Bertrand de Jouvenel, *The Art of Conjecture* (New York: Basic Books, 1967).

[7] Williams, "Inventing a Future Civilization," 139.

[8] *Ibid.*, p. 141.

[9] Peter F. Drucker, *The Age of Discontinuity* (New York: Harper and Row, 1968), p. 269.

[10] The statistical data quoted and the figures that follow are to be found in various governmental reports, primarily in "The U.S. Economy in 1980: A Preview of BLS Projections," *Monthly Labor Review*, April 1970, 3-34.

[11] Peter Milius, "Census Provides Changing Portrait of U.S. Citizens," *Los Angeles Times*, October 15, 1972, Section B, pp. 1-2.

[12] W. Vance Grant, "Education's New Scorecard," *American Education*, VIII (October 1972), 4.

[13] *Ibid.*

[14] *Ibid.*

[15] Noel Greenwood, "Schools May Contract for Teachers Training," *Los Angeles Times*, July 28, 1972, Part II, p. 1.

[16] Jack McCurdy, "2 School Reforms Ok'd by State Board," *Los Angeles Times*, April 15, 1972, p. 1.

[17] Ellsworth Mason, "The Sobering Seventies: Prospects for Change," *Library Journal*, XCVII (October 1, 1972), 3118.

[18] *Ibid.*, p. 3117.

[19] Lowell A. Martin, "The Changes Ahead," *Library Journal*, XCIII (February 15, 1968), 716.

[20] Neal Harlow, "Designs on the Curriculum," in *Education for Librarianship: The Design of the Curriculum of Library Schools*, ed. by Herbert Goldhor (Urbana, Ill.: University of Illinois, 1971), p. 16.

[21] *Ibid.*

[22] Arnold Kunzli (quoting Richard Bellman), "Towards a Qualitative Change in the Human Condition," in *Center Report* (October 1972), 3.

[23] Christopher Jenks and David Riesman, *The Academic Revolution* (Garden City, N.Y.: Doubleday, 1968), p. 206.

[24] Paul Wasserman, *The New Librarianship: A Challenge for Change* (New York: R. R. Bowker and Co., 1972), p. 134.

[25] *Ibid.*

[26] *Ibid.* p. 254.

[27] *Ibid.*

[28] Martha Jane K. Zachert, "Preparation for Special Librarianship," in

Education for Librarianship, ed. by Herbert Goldhor (Urbana, Ill.: University of Illinois, 1971), pp. 155-58.

[29] Agnes M. Griffen and John H. P. Hall, "Social Indicators and Library Change," *Library Journal*, XCVII (October 1, 1972), 3120.

[30] John Pastier, "The City as an Educational Institution," *Los Angeles Times*, July 14, 1972, Part II, p. 11.

[31] William Trombley, "College Takes New Approach ... No Grades or Majors," *Los Angeles Times*, April 17, 1972, Part II, p. 1.

[32] G. Edward Evans, "Training for Academic Librarianship: Past, Present and Future," in *Education for Librarianship*, ed. by Herbert Goldhor (Urbana, Ill.: University of Illinois, 1971), pp. 111-12.

[33] Jenks and Riesman, *The Academic Revolution*, p. 251.

BIBLIOGRAPHY

Books

Bell, Daniel. *The Reforming of General Education*. New York: Columbia University Press, 1966.

Bertin, Leonard. *Target 2067*. Toronto: Macmillan, 1968.

Drucker, Peter F. *The Age of Discontinuity*. New York: Harper and Row, 1968.

Eurich, Alvin C., ed. *Campus 1980*. New York: Delacorte Press, 1968.

Goldhor, Herbert, ed. *Education for Librarianship: The Design of the Curriculum of Library Schools*. Urbana: University of Illinois, 1971.

Jenks, Christopher, and Riesman, David. *The Academic Revolution*. Garden City, N.Y.: Doubleday & Company, 1968.

Jouvenel, Bertrand de. *The Art of Conjecture*. New York: Basic Books, 1967.

Kahn, Herman and Anthony J. Weiner. *The Year 2000*. New York: Macmillan, 1969.

Knight, Douglas M. and E. Shepley Nourse. *Libraries at Large*. New York: R.R. Bowker Company, 1969.

Lynn, Kenneth S. and the Editors of Doedalus. *The Professions in America*. Boston: Beacon Press, 1965.

Mayhew, Lewis B. *Changing Practices in Education for the Professions*. Atlanta: Southern Regional Education Board, 1971.

Silberman, Charles E. *Crisis in the Classroom; the Remaking of American Education*. New York: Random House, 1970.

Toffler, Alvin. *Future Shock*. New York: Random House, 1970.

Wilson, Logan, ed. *Emerging Patterns in American Higher Education*. Washington, D.C.: American Council on Education, 1965.

Articles

Diehl, Digby. "Q and A: Simon Ramo." *Los Angeles Times, West Magazine*, May 21, 1972.

Evans, G. Edward. "Training for Academic Librarianship." *Education for Librarianship*. Ed. by Herbert Goldhor. Urbana: University of Illinois, 1971, p. 111-12.

Grant, W. Vance. "Education's New Scoreboard." *American Education*, VIII (October 1972), 4.

Greenwood, Noel. "Schools May Contract for Teachers Training." *Los Angeles Times*, July 28, 1972, Part II, p. 1.

Griffen, Agnes M. and John H.P. Hall. "Social Indicators and Library Change." *Library Journal*, XCVII (October 1, 1972), 3120.

Harlow, Neil. "Designs on the Curriculum." *Education for Librarianship*. Ed. by Herbert Goldhor. Urbana: University of Illinois, 1971.

McCurdy, Jack. "2 School Reforms Ok'd by State Board." *Los Angeles Times*, April 15, p. 1.

Martin, Lowell A. "The Changes Ahead." *Library Journal*, XCIII (February 15, 1968), 716.

Mason, Ellsworth. "The Sobering Seventies: Prospects for Change." *Library Journal*, XCVII (October 1, 1972), 3118.

Milims, Peter. "Census Provides Changing Portrait of U.S. Citizens." *Los Angeles Times*, October 15, 1972, Section B, p. 1-2.

Pastier, John. "The City As An Educational Institution." *Los Angeles Times*, July 14, 1972, Part II, p. 11.

Trombley, William. "College Takes New Approach . . . No Grades or Majors." *Los Angeles Times*, April 17, 1972, Part II, p. 1.

Williams, Charles W. "Inventing a Future Civilization." *The Futurist*, VI (August 1972), 137-38.

Zachert, Martha Jane K. "Preparation for Special Librarianship." *Education for Librarianship*. Ed. by Herbert Goldhor. Urbana: University of Illinois, 1971, p. 155-58.

PART II

ON ANTICIPATED NEEDS

OF LIBRARIES

LIBRARY EDUCATION FOR THE FUTURE: THE SCHOOL LIBRARY

Mary Frances K. Johnson

Associate Professor
School of Education
University of North Carolina
at Greensboro

and

Phyllis J. Van Orden

Associate Professor
Graduate School of Library Service
Rutgers—The State University

Introductory Note

For the purposes of this paper, the terms "school library" and "school media center" will be used synonymously, together with the terms "school librarian" and "school media specialist."

Definitions of these and related terms are those employed in the 1969 *Standards for School Media Programs*, as follows:

Media: Printed and audiovisual forms of communication and their accompanying technology.

Media program: All the instructional and other services furnished to students and teachers by a media center and its staff.

Media center: A learning center in a school where a full range of print and audiovisual media, necessary equipment, and services from media specialists are accessible to students and teachers.

Media staff: The personnel who carry on the activities of a media center and its program.

Media specialist: An individual who has broad professional preparation in educational media. If he is responsible for instructional decisions, he meets requirements for teaching. Within this field there may be several types of specialization, such as (a) level of instruction, (b) areas of curriculum, (c) type of media, and (d) type of service. In addition other media specialists, who are not responsible for instructional decisions, are members of the professional staff and need not

29

have teacher certification, e.g., certain types of personnel in television and other media preparation areas.

Media technician: A media staff member who has training below the media specialist level, but who has special competencies in one or more of the following fields: graphics production and display, information and materials processing, photographic production, and equipment operation and simple maintenance.

Media aide: A media staff member with clerical or secretarial competencies.[1]

One further definition is derived from the report of the Commission on Instructional Technology, Committee on Education and Labor, House of Representatives:

Instructional technology: A systematic way of designing, carrying out, and evaluating the total process of learning and teaching in terms of specific objectives, based on research in human learning and communication, and employing a combination of human and non-human resources to bring about more effective instruction.[2]

Directions in Education

As an institution within an institution, the school library faces a future that will be influenced by changes occurring in the fields of librarianship and education. To prepare students to face these changes, library school educators must consider the sources of these influences.

One stable premise in school library development is that the school library exists to support and further the purposes of the school. As stated in the 1960 *Standards for School Library Programs*, "Every school library has the primary objective of contributing to the achievement of the objectives formulated by the school, of which it is an integral part."[3] It follows that the future role of the school library, or media center, is closely linked to the future role of the school it serves.

Although there is truth in Henry Brickell's assessment that "the school is a very stable institution, quite able to resist all manner of change,"[4] it is also apparent that schooling today is the object of extensive pressures *for* change. These pressures, both internal and external in origin, appear to be more numerous and pervasive than perhaps ever before.

> The world of education is not what it once was. Priorities, values, organizations, centers of power, and lines of authority are shifting radically. If old answers do not solve new problems, then we shall have to learn how to analyze the latter and rethink the former.[5]

While the concerns of those who would change the schools are diverse and often conflicting, several emphases that have much potential significance for the role of the school library and its staff can be identified. In an "inside" view of how to improve public elementary and secondary education, the National Education Association's Center for the Study of Instruction projects as a central theme (echoing Silberman) the humanistic school.

> Instructional programs aimed at developing the full range of human capacities, not just the intellectual; evaluation for the purpose of improving instruction, not for comparing children; and school organization that frees the student and the teacher to focus on learning, not the clock or the semester—these are some of the components of a humane education, an education that gives every individual a personal vision of what he might become rather than forcing him to come up to standards devised in other days for purposes that are no longer pertinent.[6]

Subsumed under the central theme of humane education are a number of imperatives as perceived by the Center for the Study of Instruction staff, including 1) "diffusion in governance" of the schools—a move away from the authoritarian model in educational systems back toward the "grass roots-based" structure; 2) relevance in curriculum; 3) approaches to classroom organization that provide for flexibility in learning environments in terms of staffing, grouping of students, instructional modes and methods, materials, facilities, and scheduling practices; 4) functional evaluation of student performance; 5) increased professionalism of the teacher, involving staff differentiation, improved preservice and continuing education, reasonable procedures for credentialing and tenure, and appropriate teacher responsibility and control, or accountability; and 6) learner-directed instruction, focused on the needs of the individual.[7]

> At a minimum, humane education demands schooling tailored for each individual—a flexible educational program that can accommodate differences in ability to learn, readiness for learning, learning styles, social and emotional maturity, and other traits that distinguish one young human from another and that affect his scholastic performance.[8]

To these concerns and recommendations might be added another: the emphasis on "learning how to learn." Viewed by the Educational Policies Commission in 1961 as "the central purpose in education,"[9] this goal and its importance have been recognized widely.[10] Frances Henne, in "Learning to Learn in School Libraries," discussed the role of the school library in supporting this emphasis in education, concluding as follows:

> Inquiry, independent or individual study, and self-directed learning occupy a strong position in the philosophy of modern education, and in this development the school library's resources and its program of teaching study and research skills form a key and integral part at all levels of elementary and secondary education.[11]

Concerns and recommendations for the improvement of the schools such as those enumerated above support, at least philosophically, a broader potential role for the school library and, in application, generate increased demand for library service. They also challenge many traditional assumptions about school library service, increasing the pressure for redefinition of its roles and practices. It should be recognized, further, that some approaches springing into vogue as means by which to accomplish new emphases in education may serve, in some times and places, to disrupt or even displace the library; some implementations

31

of the "British primary school" concepts in this country may furnish examples.[12]

Other forces widely recognized as affecting the potential of the school library include 1) the knowledge "explosion," generating demands for broader instructional resources in the schools; 2) the proliferation of instructional materials, both in terms of media formats available and the rate of their production/publication; 3) increased utilization of audiovisual hardware and communications systems, such as closed-circuit television (CC/TV), cable television (CATV), and the video tape recorder (VTR), in instruction; 4) the instructional technology movement, reflected in the use of programmed instruction (PI), individually prescribed instruction (IPI), computer-assisted instruction (CAI), and other systematic approaches to the design of instruction; and 5) the growth of educational systems: reorganization of school districts, development of district-level media services, cooperative programs, networks, etc.

The growth of educational systems appears to be accelerating, despite the call of the NEA's Center for the Study of Instruction to return to the "grass roots" base in governance. However, counter trends are found in the development of alternative schools and other varieties of non-public schools; experiments based on proposals for using educational voucher systems with parents and students selecting their schools; and approaches to decentralization of control of urban school systems. Another approach is suggested by the "educational park" concept of the school. Writing in *Futurist*, Congressman Phillip Burton describes the school of tomorrow as:

> ... an integral part of the community. It will be constructed with community needs in mind and designed flexibly enough to meet these needs. Its facilities: library, medical, recreational, as well as its multi-purpose class areas will serve the community and make the school of tomorrow a focal point in the community life for old and young alike.
>
> The school will no longer be the part-time establishment operating eight to four, five days a week, nine and one-half months a year.[13]

In considering changes that are probable or possible or desirable in the schools of the future, it is important to recognize not only that opinions differ, rather than representing a united front, but also that schools develop on a "broken front." That is, different, even conflicting, approaches and different stages of development can be found everywhere: within a classroom, between classrooms, between schools, in different localities. This diversity reinforces Brickell's analysis of the difficulty of effecting change in education.[14] Still another implication emerges from the diversity of educational practice: the school media center and its staff must respond to differing demands and expectations, individualizing work not only with students but also with teachers, while promoting and assisting changes in practices viewed as undesirable.

Although change is uneven, it seems clear that the pace of change in schools is accelerating. An example is found in the development of national standards for school library/media service. *School Libraries for Today and Tomorrow*, published in 1945,[15] was replaced in 1960 by *Standards for School Library*

Programs,[16] and the release of quantitative standards for audiovisual services, by the Department of Audiovisual Instruction, National Education Association, followed in 1966.[17] *Standards for School Media Programs*, prepared and issued jointly by the American Association of School Librarians (AASL) and the Department of Audiovisual Instruction (DAVI), was published in 1969, with a prefatory note stating that ". . . significant social changes, educational developments, and technological innovations have made it imperative to present new statements of standards," and adding that "because of the rapidity of change in educational, technological, and other fields, the Joint Committee recognizes that national standards require continuous revision, and recommends that such revisions be made at least biennially."[18] Work on standards revision and development was conducted during 1971 and 1972, with task forces from both AASL and the Association for Educational Communications and Technology (formerly DAVI) participating in the revision of building-level standards (Task Force I) and the development of standards for media programs at school district levels (Task Force II). Publication of the two sets of new standards is anticipated in 1973.

Possible implications of these directions in education for the school library of the future are explored in the next part of this paper.

The School Library of the Future

Given the context in which the school library operates, as a subsystem of the school, and the diversity that is characteristic of schools today, predictions concerning the emerging role of the school library and its professional staff cannot claim to be more than tentative hypotheses, considering the numerous variables and the difficulty of achieving adequate perspective. The suggestions that follow, then, are offered only as a limited view of significant features of the school library of the future, characteristics that in turn have significant implications for the professional education of school librarians.

One prediction should be relatively safe: *media center collections will continue to broaden in scope*, in response to the needs of students and teachers for convenient access to a multiplicity of materials and related equipment in a variety of media formats. It is to be expected that increased use will be made of materials in some of the newer media formats such as programed instruction (brief topics in text form), video tape recordings, manipulative materials in various forms, educational games and simulation materials, even consumables. It is to be hoped that the traditional barriers separating "textbooks" from "library resources" (in the eyes of teachers and librarians) will disappear. Increased demand is anticipated for locally produced materials ranging from overhead transparencies to "learning centers" to "learning activity packages" for self-directed use by students. With the range of options increasing steadily, along with stimulus from developments in curriculum and instruction for fuller exploitation of these options, the demand will grow for media specialists with a high level of competency in the characteristics and utilization of the range of instructional resources.

It should follow that *a broader scope and range of media services* will be required to respond to the needs of students and teachers, as well as *the redirection of some traditional services.* The provision of graphics and other media production facilities and services as a part of the media center operation has been effected today in many schools, with rapid and favorable response. Demands continue to grow for such audiovisual support systems as video tape recording and closed circuit television production services. The long-standing objective of guiding students in "reading, listening, and viewing" is being served by new approaches with emphasis on individualization of programming, provision of options, "hands-on" experiences, relevance to students, involvement. The journals feature descriptions of media production by students as means to self-discovery; of "visual literacy" or "mediacy" programs sponsored by the media center; of learning centers designed by librarians to serve individual and small-group exploration and learning. Both the school environment and technological advances bring into question some of the traditional ways of doing things. The class group is increasingly suspect as the "unit" for reading guidance experiences at the elementary school level; the open classroom does not generate passive audiences. In another example, the old debate about the role of reference services (to inform—i.e., to provide the needed information or sources—vs. to educate—i.e., to teach the skills of using library resources) is renewed. Increased support for advocates of the information services function arises from our growing capability to provide information, on the one hand, and the changing emphasis in school assignments (from retrieval of facts to questions of causes and relationships), on the other. The expansion and redirection of media programs of services underscores the values of differentiated staffing and raises questions for the education of media specialists—e.g., what level of competence is needed to direct a visual literacy program? How many areas of special competence—in media formats, in depth of subject matter knowledge, in types of services to students and teachers—can be expected of one media professional? How might options be extended for students who wish to develop special interests and skills? What areas constitute bona fide specializations—ideally and/or in relation to actual and potential job opportunities?

A related concern now receiving increased attention is the *individualization of programming* in media services, with such attendant emphases as improved techniques for diagnosis of the individual learner's needs, awareness of alternatives from which to select what is appropriate for an individual or group, design of self-instructional approaches to learning library and study skills, and increasing the accessibility of the media center through flexibility in scheduling. "Basic" competencies in theories of learning and in the approaches to systematic instructional design seem imperative for the school librarian of the future. Designing preparation programs that develop such competencies calls for the interdisciplinary efforts of specialists in learning, curriculum and instruction, and librarianship.

A highly important role for the media center professional is that of *serving as consultant to teachers*. This role has been advocated and described over a number of years by Henne, Graham, Grazier, and others,[19] and is given considerable emphasis in both the 1960 and the 1969 standards. It remains in practice a role performed too seldom and/or too inadequately, in many schools, due both to a low level of teacher expectations of media services and insufficient personnel on the media center staff to accomplish the needed functions. In the "mainstream" library as described by Margaret Grazier,[20] the school librarian is an active and informed participant in the planning of curriculum, assignments, and approaches to instruction. This role, as indicated above, is not suggested to be a new one; however, it raises several questions for library education in the future: Are school librarians being prepared adequately for their function in promoting and upgrading media utilization? To what extent is the nature of their work with teachers in curriculum planning shaped or limited by their preparation in various subject fields?[21] Is the preparation of school librarians even minimally adequate for designing and conducting inservice education programs for teachers? What is the distinction between the "assistance in planning curriculum and assignments" function and that of instructional technology, the latter requiring specialization of a different order? Further, the role of the teacher is changing from that of directing students collectively to that of serving as guide and facilitator of the individual student's learning experience. "If the teacher is to direct learning toward inquiry, he must himself remain an inquirer."[22] This shift in the role of the teacher changes the teacher's and the student's use of the school library, and the ways in which the school librarian works with both—a new level (if not kind) of involvement in instruction. The librarian, too, must "remain an inquirer."

Closely related to the preceding function and of critical importance for the school library of the future (indeed, *to* its future) is *the responsibility for "conceptualizing," interpreting, and demonstrating the role of the media program* and the media specialist in the school. Again, the problems of inadequate conceptualization of the role and difficulty in describing and clarifying it to other educators and laymen are not new.[23] The essentials of the school library program seem almost to defy description, except by example, of which Gaver's recent study affords the most complete enumeration.[24] (The 1960 standards listed areas of function and services in an approach more specific, if more limited, than that provided in the 1969 standards.) This problem in the dissemination and adoption of the media program as recommended in national standrads was pinpointed by Brickell, in his discussion of the dynamics of educational change and the size of the task faced in implementing *Standards for School Media Programs*:

> . . . . I doubt that the description of the media program is adequate as a description. I do not think the user can picture what you mean. He can picture the equipment and books, I suppose, but I do not think he can picture the human behaviors that you are calling for. There is a serious question in my mind as to whether you can stick to one medium in communicating this very important message. It may be that for the human behaviors you would like to describe, print is not a very good medium. The user cannot adopt what he cannot picture. He literally cannot know whether he has it or not.[25]

Thus the dilemma. Few school librarians escape the imperative to stimulate interest and develop awareness, on the part of teachers, of the contributions of media services to instruction—in most cases with insufficient staff to deliver a full range of services. Nevertheless, the building of demand must be given priority, along with inservice education efforts to extend teacher competence in media utilization. Walker's study of student teachers' knowledge and expectations of the school library concluded:

> .... The overwhelming frequency of responses regarding the value of the library as a source of materials for research, supplemental reading, and recreational reading materials, highlights the tendency of student teachers to view the library as a place where students can get ready to learn, or to reinforce what they have already learned, but not a place where they gain new learning.[26]

In the long range, efforts by the practitioner must be accompanied by leadership from the library profession to improve teacher preparation in media utilization, which has been the subject of considerable expert attention[27] but too little effective action. Saddler's study of textbooks used in college courses in teacher education revealed a very limited level of inclusion of any content in library and media use,[28] while Van Orden's analysis of the content of professional journals for elementary school teachers reached similar conclusions.[29] Still more discouraging is the infrequency with which professional materials developed to assist teachers in implementing new approaches to curriculum and instruction give attention to media services and their role. Cases in point appear to be many of the publications on the open classroom, as well as print materials to guide teachers in schools participating in the I/D/E/A-sponsored program for "Individually Guided Education" (IGE)—although this project has released an excellent film, "Many Roads," demonstrating patterns of use of the media center. Rather than continuing to leave to the practitioner efforts to upgrade teachers' expectations and utilization of media, library education programs need to exert greater influence for improvement of preservice and inservice education of teachers. This position is supported by resolutions adopted by the Association for Supervision and Curriculum Development[30] and the American Association of School Librarians.[31]

The concept of *staff differentiation* within the media center is gaining support from many sources and levels. Applications in current practice range from a new acceptance of the importance of utilizing both paid and volunteer aides to increased demand for the employment of a full range of media professionals having varied and complementary specializations, technicians (likewise varied), and support staff. Limitations in financial support and reductions in sources that can support media center staffing, in some cases, are presently retarding the expansion of differentiated staffing in school media centers, but the trend is expected to continue in response to urgent needs for such staffing.

Such factors as the growing complexity of media collections and services and the implementation of differentiated staffing underscore the necessity for the school librarian to possess *competence in management functions*. In the school library of the future, professional staff members will need to assist in the selection of support staff, prepare job definitions and descriptions, provide on-the-job training, supervise and evaluate job performance. Equally important, they must demonstrate skills in interpersonal relationships in order to function effectively as members of a team of professional media specialists with complementary roles, while additional competencies in personnel management

36

will be required of the professional designated as "head" of the school media center. The growth of district-level, cooperative, and commercial services, whose impact on what can and should be performed at the school building level must be assessed, represents still another factor that increases the need for management skills. Education for school librarianship must shift in focus, if it has not already done so, from a "how to do it" (one way) approach to a broader context. A base in skills and techniques is still needed, but of at least equal importance is an awareness of options and an appreciation of the relationship of means to ends—the capability to shape procedures and services to respond to the particular characteristics of the school, the instructional program, and the population served.

Finally, *increasing diversity* is predicted in the school media centers of the future, as the individual center responds more fully to the particular goals, emphases, instructional approaches, and student population in the school it serves. Although common functions should persist, the specifics of means by which they are performed may be significantly different and varied. This diversity, reflecting the multiplicity that exists in schools' approaches to curriculum and instruction, is viewed as positive in effect and a necessary response to the enlarged responsibilities assumed by the school library. It is in keeping with the views expressed in *Schools for the 70's and Beyond*:

> Perhaps the greatest barrier to educational improvement is the tendency of educational reformers to say, "That's wrong; do it this way." Any method of educating, even the much-maligned self-contained classroom, is right as long as some teacher and some group of students can make it work. Rather than prescribing a single solution for every educational malady, a wise teacher considers every option available to him—what John Goodlad once referred to as "the entire pharmacy of educational alternatives." In this spirit, the Center for the Study of Instruction chooses not to dictate solutions but to present alternatives. . . .[32]

It follows that library education programs need to learn more about how to identify, attract, and develop persons capable of such professional judgments.

Challenges in Library Education

Predictions about the future role of the school library give rise to a number of questions about our present capability to prepare staff for these libraries. Harlow summed up the challenge as follows: "To know our objectives; to accept only persons who are capable of full professional service; to educate them as intellectuals; and to employ them as librarians—this prescription will cure some of our most chronic professional staffing problems."[33]

A major issue is the means by which to distinguish, in curriculum planning, what is essential from what may be "nice to know." It is a question of values and objectives, and ultimately a problem of achieving adequate job definitions. Contributions to the latter task have been made in the work of Asheim,[34] the School Library Manpower Project,[35] and the Jobs in Media Study (JIMS).[36] Library education curricula (as well as the total program for the preparation of the school librarian) need to avoid several traps: education for the past, based on outmoded views of the school librarian's role; narrowly prescriptive programs leading to rigidity rather than flexibility in practices—and which may freeze students into given types of positions in conflict with the trends relating to job mobility and career lattices; and the "smattering" approach which emphasizes breadth at the expense of depth and results in superficiality. Striking an appropriate balance calls for the best available information on the critical tasks to be performed by the school librarian, and a new level of competence, on the part of library educators, to establish and apply valid admissions criteria, to assess comptencies achieved by students, to evaluate program in terms of demonstrated performance, to test alternatives—in short, to demonstrate "accountability."

A related question concerns appropriate provision for specialization and staff differentiation, within library education programs. Several factors may discourage such provisions. Increasing job mobility, for example, challenges narrow specialization of roles, as do our inadequate knowledge of future directions and the growing diversity among schools, while the greatest demand among present jobs is for the "media generalist" or head of the school media center, with proportionately few positions established for other professional specialists. (Staff differentiation today appears to be effected most often at the level of providing support staff.) While a single "generalist" program for preparing the school librarian seems less and less tenable, serious consideration must be given to what constitutes valid specialization within this field.

Institutional constraints that serve as barriers to improvement of library education cannot be ignored. One set of problems arises from the large number and variety of programs for the education of school librarians, programs that differ widely in administrative placement (autonomous departments, programs attached to education departments, unified library/media programs); in level of preparation offered; in institutional support and commitment as measured in faculty, budget, etc. The diversity in programs, apparent from examination of the latest national survey findings,[37] reflects uneven capabilities of the programs and makes for difficulty in effective communication and cooperation at any higher level—area, state, regional, or national. Other problems may be found (or perceived) within graduate library schools with multipurpose programs, which have been subject to criticism by the school library profession on such grounds as relatively low priority given to the school librarian program, faculty, and students; inadequate specialization in curriculum; and limited representation of faculty specialists in education, school librarianship, and newer media.

Other problems common in higher education and having special significance for the education of school librarians include the difficulties often encountered in cooperative action between separate departments or schools. Built-in handicaps to program development may be found on campuses with established separate library education and audiovisual education or instructional technology units. Interaction between separate teacher education and library education departments may be difficult to establish or sustain. Yet the preparation of the school librarian of the future calls for effective integration of these program components. Another serious problem is found in the limited provision of resources (human and material) needed for adequate instructional support in the education of school librarians—e.g., instructional materials for children and young people, including trade books, textbooks, and audiovisual materials; related audiovisual equipment accessible for individual use; laboratories for training students in equipment operation and materials production techniques; consultant service from specialists in instructional development. Widespread inadequacies in the provision of such instructional resources are suggested in the first report of the Educational Media Selection Centers Program,[38] while the Carnegie Commission on Higher Education in its report on instructional technology urges that priority be given to encouraging and supporting higher education faculty members in the development of instructional materials and the utilization of technologies of instruction.[39]

Adequate communication and cooperation between the campus and the field must be effected. The relatively recent development of school libraries, in many areas, and the wide range in their quality present challenges to the development of cooperative approaches in the preparation of school librarians, but the potential benefits are mutual and significant: provision of appropriate field experiences as integral components of library education programs; maintenance of faculty awareness of current developments; improvement of school library programs. A related need, augmented by the rapid pace of change, is to clarify the complementary roles of preservice and continuing education; to build awareness among prospective school librarians of the necessity for continuing education; and to extend the role of library education programs, working in cooperation with school systems, in providing continuing education opportunities for practitioners.

The Future of Library Education: Tasks and Approaches

As implied in the preceding discussion, the problem faced in developing more adequate programs for educating school librarians is *not* to produce a set of prescriptions for the one right way all programs should go, but rather to identify and implement approaches that will contribute to the desired end. What seems appropriate, then, is consideration of tasks that lie ahead and approaches to their accomplishment that may be undertaken at various levels, national, state, and local.

National Level

A major continuing task is the development and "maintenance" of sound occupational definitions, reflecting the emerging roles of school media professionals and keeping pace with the implementation of specializations and staff differentiation. Significant efforts have been made in this direction, e.g., the Library Education and Manpower policy statement adopted in June 1970 by the ALA Council;[40] the task analysis survey conducted by the School Library Manpower Project[41] (although the design of this study has been questioned); the occupational definitions developed by the School Library Manpower Project;[42] as well as the Jobs in Media Study (JIMS) conducted by the Association for Educational Communications and Technology.[43] Still, further work is needed to refine such statements and to keep pace with developing roles in school library service. Valid, current, comprehensive definitions provide a base for program planning, contributing both to the establishment of objectives and to influencing employment practices. While work on such definitions is required at every level, leadership in this effort at the national level seems particularly appropriate in order to achieve broad, informed perspective on the roles of school media professionals and to provide maximum capability for wide dissemination of findings and recommendations. It should be added that defining the roles of school media professionals is not suggested to be a task for library education programs to perform unilaterally, bur rather a responsibility of all segments of the profession, one of critical importance to the improvement of education for school librarians.

Continued work is needed on guidelines for professional education, both as a part of the larger context of education for librarianship and with specific reference to education of school librarians. Also needed is continuing attention to guidelines for teacher education, including appropriate teacher education components in the preparation of school librarians and, also, improved preparation of teachers in effective media utilization. These topics will not be considered further here, except for identification of a problem with respect to standards and accreditation that relates specifically to the preparation of school librarians. Questions arise concerning the roles and relationships of the American Library Association (ALA) and the National Commission for Accreditation of Teacher Education (NCATE) in the areas of standards and accreditation. Numerous programs for education of school librarians now operate without ALA accreditation. Should such programs—both undergraduate and graduate— continue to exist?[44] Can the ALA develop the capability to evaluate them for accreditation, if this is sought, and (if so) should the ALA attempt this job? Do the new ALA Standards for Accreditation apply as appropriately to unified programs for the preparation of school librarians and other instructional media specialists, as they do to unified library science/information science programs? How "acceptable is ALA accreditation to other professional groups concerned with school media service, such as the Association for Educational Communications and Technology? What role might NCATE play in the evaluation and accreditation of programs for the education of school librarians as media specialists? The latter is a subject often viewed with alarm, but one that seems worthy of consideration. The present situation may be viewed as a "stand-off": since ALA is empowered to accredit library education, NCATE abstains. Yet ALA has not really implemented the accreditation of "single-purpose" programs. In one sense such programs are in limbo, although there is some evidence that NCATE is ambivalent in practice. (In the university in which one of these writers teaches, the unified program in library education/instructional media, a program area of the School of Education, was included by request in the university's self-study report for NCATE accreditation purposes, was reviewed by the NCATE visiting committee, and was included in that committee's final report—perhaps because of its association with "newer media." Other such instances have been reported.) It appears that further attention by ALA and NCATE is needed to matters of jurisdiction. Another factor for consideration here is the growing use by state departments of education of reciprocity agreements by means of which graduates of out-of-state programs are granted certification in other states. Graduation from an NCATE-approved program

40

serves as one basis for reciprocity.[45] Since certification is a requirement for the public school librarian, an advantage offered by NCATE approval of programs is currently withheld from school librarians. There must be a way out, with good will and cooperative planning. The proposal for a national conference on certification, submitted in 1972 by the American Association of School Librarians for the J. Morris Jones—World Book Encyclopedia—ALA Goals Award, although not selected for funding, represents an approach to national dialogue on this subject deserving further consideration. Again, these suggestions concern action that transcends library education programs *per se*, but to which they can contribute support and assistance.

Other important national efforts are those that provide impetus for curriculum revision and program development, in such forms as national attention, consultant help, guidelines, and financial support. Here the six experimental programs being conducted during 1971-73 with support from the School Library Manpower Project[46] represent a promising approach, while other approaches needed in higher education generally are outlined by the Carnegie Commission on Higher Education.[47] More such efforts and more nationwide dialogue are needed. The verdict seems less clear, at least to these writers, concerning the contribution to curriculum revision made by the HEA, II-B (formerly NDEA) institute program conducted by the U.S. Office of Education. Although the funding provided for institutes has been beneficial in many ways, it can be argued that it has contributed less to curriculum revision and development than to general program building (recruitment of standards, program recognition, enrichment of experiences provided, etc.). It is possible that the work of developing institute proposals and conducting institutes has been diversionary in effect, in some cases, withdrawing faculty energies from systematic curriculum development. Certainly there is the risk of inappropriate shaping of an institution's program to fit federal priorities. These speculations are not offered in protest against the institute program, which has obviously made important contributions to library education for school librarians, but rather to suggest that other, more open-ended approaches are also needed to support curriculum development. Similarly, the HEA, II-B fellowship program provided limited guarantees of impact on program development (and, as administered by some graduate library schools, drew criticism for the limited contribution made by fellowships to the graduate preparation of school library personnel). A significant federal approach was represented by the U.S. Office of Education Bureau of Research request for proposals for "Educational Specifications for a Comprehensive Undergraduate and Inservice Teacher Education Program for Elementary Teachers." The nine teacher education models funded used systems analysis to develop their program specifications. Common characteristics of the projects include individualized instruction, establishment of behavioral objectives, development of human relations skills, utilization of technology for instructional purposes, and education for teachers beyond the first four years of college.[48] Many aspects of these model programs are applicable to library education.

Shera's recommendations for the improvement of education for librarianship lend support to the views outlined above:

The author, therefore, concludes that improved education for librarianship does not need research so much as it needs support for the building of a strong faculty, the attraction of outstanding students, and the resources for experimentation. Particularly important is the need to strengthen the dialogue with scholars in related subject disciplines so that the results of their innovations and discoveries can be applied to library education. (Abstract)[49]

Another continuing need at the national level is strengthened efforts to promote effective communication among the diverse groups—programs, agencies, and associations—concerned with the education of school librarians. More effective means are needed to facilitate exchange of program information and to promote state and regional planning. Given the varying kinds of institutional structures in which programs for educating school librarians exist, no one channel for communication now seems to reach everybody effectively.

A final issue for consideration is the placement (level) and scope (duration) of programs for the education of school librarians. The long-standing debate within the profession (largely school librarians vs. other librarians) was reopened with fervor upon the adoption of the ALA Library Education and Manpower policy statement, and seems likely to continue. It is in part an artificial issue, as colleges and universities relax restrictions concerning the grade levels of studies, and as we try seriously to implement competency-based programs which demand that students demonstrate achievement of program objectives. Nevertheless, it persists as a matter of very real and practical consequences as long as different levels of college degrees are offered and different levels of certification (and of employment opportunities) based on these degrees prevail. As suggested by Grazier,[50] it would seem that no less time is required for the adequate preparation of the school librarian than for professionals in other fields of library service. The demands of the position may indeed be higher, in terms of preparation, due to the breadth of competencies required and the skills in interpersonal relationships that must be brought to bear in work with teachers and students. Further support for five-year programs comes from recognition of comparable requirements for professionals in other fields, and from the widely-recognized need to upgrade the status of the librarian within the school. The opposition by segments of the school library profession to the policy statement on Library Education and Manpower can be criticized as a short-range view, one that has damaged the image and status of the professional school librarian and contributed to divisiveness within librarianship. But to criticize is not enough. Further attention to this issue is needed at the national level, both to influence the programs that prepare school library personnel and the agencies that set certification guidelines, and to guide prospective school librarians and employing agencies. Such study should give continuing consideration to the place of/need for undergraduate preparation of personnel for preprofessional, "entry-level" roles; fifth-year (or five-year) programs; and advanced programs for sixth-year and doctoral study.

State Level
Foremost among the needs at the state level is a long-recognized but still too

seldom realized goal: the development of some agency, body, or mechanism through which state-wide planning for library education can be effected. This need, common to all programs in library education, is augmented for programs preparing school librarians by the sheer number of such programs. A mechanism for meaningful state-wide planning, transcending the separateness of individual institutions and providing adequately for representation of practitioners, deserves priority as an effort for state planning. Library education programs can interpret this need and promote the development of means for state-wide planning.

Another area of need, in which progress is being made, is the adoption of more flexible guidelines for the certification of professionals in education, including school librarians. Despite the criticisms of Broudy and others,[51] guidelines such as those recently adopted in North Carolina[52] appear to offer opportunity for considerably greater flexibility in the design and implementation of programs, reducing the artificial constraints concerning credit hours and areas of study long typical of certification regulations. A related concern at the state level is the implementation of interstate compacts for reciprocity in certification, an approach promoted by the National Association of State Directors of Teacher Education Certification (NASDTEC).

Individual Program Level

No easy answers, no finite "solutions" present themselves in answer to questions about curriculum reform and program development in the individual higher education program for the education of school librarians. What seems valid is recommendations concerning certain program characteristics that are perceived as values in higher education generally, and others relating to the process by which sound programs can be developed.

General values sought increasingly in higher education include flexibility and individualization of programs, achieved by program designs and instructional approaches that extend the student's options in such respects as selection of content components and pacing of work and that provide for improved assessment of the individual student's competencies. Other such values include the establishment of clearly-defined priorities guiding program development and the concern for "accountability," in which program components are evaluated rigorously for contribution to program goals.

Concerning "process," considerable promise is seen in a systematic approach to instructional development—a move from the traditional course addition/ deletion model in curriculum development to a "systems" model or approach. Application of systematic instructional development demands, at the least, 1) role analysis and definition, 2) identification of competencies required for the roles served by media specialists and agreement on priorities within these, 3) design of curriculum and instruction to achieve the competencies sought, and 4) development of means for assessing competencies and evaluating program effectiveness in achieving them. Such an approach, admittedly difficult and demanding, has merit in promoting thoroughgoing reexamination of present programs.

Another general concern in program development is the concept of cooperative approaches to program planning and implementation. It is unlikely

43

that the "self-contained" program can continue to be accepted as a viable approach. It never has been accepted, in the context of basic areas—general studies, subject specialization, teacher education, and library education—that contribute to the preparation of school librarians. Now it becomes unlikely, or inappropriate (in terms of duplication), or undesirable (in terms of relative competency) for even the library education segment to "go it alone." Cooperation here is viewed as more extensive than relying on another department or school for a required course; the essential features of team teaching—joint responsibility by a designated group for establishing objectives, planning instruction, assigning students, providing instruction, and evaluation of results—are what is needed. Sound curricula for the school librarian of the future require, for example, adequate inputs from competent specialists in such fields as learning, developmental psychology, curriculum and teaching, and instructional technology.

A related need is the provision of adequate staffing for education programs and the achievement of flexibility in staff deployment. Team teaching, for example, can break down rapidly under the burden of inflexible formulas by which faculty loads are assigned and assessed, or the different formulas by which summer session faculty are employed and assigned. Although the problems and needs here are common to all areas of higher education, they have particular urgency in programs for education of school librarians in view of the complexity and interdisciplinary nature of the role school librarians are assuming.

Still another related need is the achievement of greater flexibility in approaches to instruction, again an area in which institutional constraints have often inhibited change. Much attention is being given to the use of modular approaches to curriculum building,[53] rather than to approach all learning in terms of units of 2 or 3 credits. A companion trend is to the wider utilization of varied strategies of instruction, emphasizing use of modular scheduling; individualized instruction; self-instruction components; techniques such as case studies, role playing, simulation games, microteaching; more involvement of students in planning and evaluation of learning experiences; emphasis, in group instruction, on problem-solving experiences rather than teacher presentation; small group learning experiences that foster interaction. Awareness of the options possible and understanding of their potential, in relation to objectives, content, and students, are attributes that need cultivation.

Our experiences and assessments of the effectiveness of different methods and materials need to be shared. Individuals in library education who have interest in developing new instructional materials, such as simulation games and programmed instructional materials, need to be encouraged and supported. Opportunities for inservice and continuing education of library educators should be extended.

The various influences affecting elementary and secondary education, outlined earlier in this paper, may serve as sources of content for the curriculum of the future—e.g., more attention to the school as an institution and to its political and sociological environment. Opportunities are needed for students to understand the "change" process; engage in decision-making processes; grow in awareness of themselves and openness to others; justify their viewpoints in discussion settings; experience varied teaching/learning patterns and engage in analysis of these; examine varied professional opportunities and roles found in the school library setting; and test themselves in varied types of school settings to extend understanding of their own needs, interests, and abilities.

The relationship of the campus to the field, of professor to practitioner, is the subject of growing attention both in teacher education and in library education, reflected in increased provision for field experience components in library education, in more discussion about the role of higher education programs in influencing practices in the field, in more involvement of practitioners in advisory roles to library education programs, in more demand for follow-up studies to assess graduates' performance on the job and, thereby, program effectiveness.

Conclusion

The task of developing sound programs for educating the school librarians of the future calls for the combined efforts of specialists in librarianship, education, learning, and instructional development, working effectively with practitioners, professional associations, and other agencies that can help to effect changes in the roles and career opportunities of school media personnel. Means must be sought to provide impetus and support for curriculum development; to improve and extend communication and cooperation among the individual library education programs; and to achieve effective "quality control" of programs. Essential program characteristics include clear definition of objectives and priorities, modular approaches to curriculum design, appropriate utilization of varied instructional methods, including technology, and provision for flexibility and individualization in program components.

FOOTNOTES

[1] American Association of School Librarians and Department of Audio-visual Instruction, *Standards for School Media Programs* (Chicago: American Library Association; Washington: National Education Association, 1969), p. xv.

[2] Commission on Instructional Technology, *To Improve Learning: An Evaluation of Instructional Technology*. Sidney G. Tickton, ed. (New York: Bower, 1970), I, p. 22.

[3] American Association of School Librarians, *Standards for School Library Programs* (Chicago: American Library Association, 1960), p. 8.

[4] Henry M. Brickell, "Implementing Educational Change," *School Libraries*, XIX (Summer 1970), 20.

[5] Neil P. Atkins, "Introduction," in *Curricular Concerns in a Revolutionary Era*, ed. by Robert R. Leeper (Washington: Association for Supervision and Curriculum Development, 1971), p. x.

[6] National Education Association. Center for the Study of Instruction, *Schools for the 70's and Beyond: A Call to Action* (Washington: National Education Association, 1971), p. 71.

[7] *Ibid.*

[8] *Ibid.*, p. 94.

[9] Educational Policies Commission, *The Central Purpose of American Education* (Washington: National Education Association, 1961).

[10] Ruth Ann Davies, *The School Library: A Force for Educational Excellence* (New York: Bowker, 1970). Also, Herbert Kohl, *The Open Classroom* (New York: Random House, 1970); National Education Association. Project on the Instructional Program of the Public Schools, *Deciding What to Teach* (Washington: National Education Association, 1963); and Charles E. Silberman, *Crisis in the Classroom; The Remaking of American Education* (New York: Random House, 1970).

[11] Frances Henne, "Learning to Learn in School Libraries," *School Libraries*, XV (May 1966), 15-17.

[12] Evelyn Geller, "So Near and Yet So Far: Libraries and Open Schools," *School Library Journal*, XVIII (February 1972), 40-44; and Gertrude Herman, "The Open Corridor Schools and the Library," *School Library Journal*, XIX (September 1972), 36-40.

[13] Phillip Burton, "Education Tomorrow," *The Futurist*, III (December 1969), 150.

[14] Brickell, "Implementing Educational Change," 20.

[15] American Library Association. Committee on Post-War Planning, *School Libraries for Today and Tomorrow; Functions and Standards* (Chicago: American Library Association, 1945).

[16] American Association of School Librarians, *Standards for School Library Programs.*

[17] National Education Association. Department of Audiovisual Instruction, *Quantitative Standards for Audiovisual Personnel, Equipment and Materials in Elementary, Secondary, and Higher Education* (Washington: the Department, 1966). (Mimeographed.)

[18] American Association of School Librarians and Department of Audiovisual Instruction, *Standards for School Media Programs*, pp. ix, xi.

[19] Frances Henne, "The Challenge of Change—New Standards for New Times," *Bulletin of the National Association of Secondary-School Principals*, L (January 1966), 75-81; Margaret Hayes Grazier, "The High School Library in Transition" (Chicago: American Association of School Librarians, Knapp School Libraries Project, 1967). (Mimeographed.); Margaret Hayes Grazier, "The Library and New Programs," *The Bulletin of the National Association of Secondary-School Principals*, L (January 1966), 18-24; Ruth Ann Davies, *The School Library*; Mary V. Gaver, *Services of Secondary School Media Centers: Evaluation and Development* (Chicago: American Library Association, 1971); and Mae Graham, ed., "The Changing Nature of the School Library," *Library Trends* XVII (April 1969), 343-433.

[20] Grazier, "The Library and New Programs."

[21] *Ibid.*

[22] Ole Sand, *On Staying Awake: Talks with Teachers* (Washington: National Education Association, Center for the Study of Instruction, 1970), p. 14.

[23] Jesse H. Shera, "Staffing Library Services to Meet Student Needs—Library Education," in *Student Use of Libraries; An Inquiry into the Needs of*

Students, Libraries, and the Educational Process (Chicago: American Library Association, 1964), pp. 122-33.

[24] Gaver, *Services of Secondary School Media Centers.*

[25] Brickell, "Implementing Educational Change," 21.

[26] Jerry Walker, "What Do Student Teachers Know About Libraries?" *School Libraries*, XVI (Winter 1967), 18.

[27] Paul W. F. Witt, "Preservice Education of Teachers in the Selection and Use of All Types of Instructional Materials with Implications for the Library," in *The School Library as a Materials Center*, ed. by Mary Helen Mahar (Washington: U.S. Department of Health, Education and Welfare, Office of Education, 1964); *idem.*, "Teacher Education and School Libraries," *School Libraries*, XIV (October 1964), 37-46; *Audiovisual Instruction*, XIV (January 1969). (Issue devoted to teacher education in media); Commission on Instructional Technology, *To Improve Learning*; and Carnegie Commission on Higher Education, *The Fourth Revolution; Instructional Technology in Higher Education* (New York: McGraw-Hill, 1972).

[28] Virginia B. Saddler, "Role of the Library in Education" (unpublished manuscript, Barbourville, Kentucky, 1970).

[29] Phyllis Jeanne Van Orden, "Use of Media and the Media Center, as Reflected in Professional Journals for Elementary School Teachers" (unpublished Ed.D. dissertation, Wayne State University, 1970).

[30] "Encouraging Instruction in the Use of Instructional Materials" (Washington: Association for Supervision and Curriculum Development, 1958). (Mimeographed.)

[31] "To Promote Competency of Use of Library Resources" (Chicago: American Association of School Librarians, 1960). (Mimeographed.)

[32] National Education Association. Center for the Study of Instruction, *Schools for the 70's and Beyond*, p. 22.

[33] Neal Harlow, "Commentary," in *Student Use of Libraries*, p. 136.

[34] Lester E. Asheim, "Education and Manpower for Librarianship: First Steps Toward a Statement of Policy," *ALA Bulletin*, LXII (October 1968), 1096-1106.

[35] American Association of School Librarians. School Library Manpower Project, *Occupational Definitions for School Library Media Personnel* (Chicago: American Library Association, 1971).

[36] C. James Wallington and others, eds., *Jobs in Instructional Media* (Washington: Association for Educational Communications and Technology, 1970).

[37] *North American Library Education; Directory and Statistics, 1969-1971*. Frank L. Schick and D. Kathryn Weintraub, eds. (Chicago: American Library Association, 1972).

[38] John Rowell and M. Ann Heidbreder, *Educational Media Selection Centers: Identification and Analysis of Current Practices* (Chicago: American Library Association, 1971).

[39] Carnegie Commission on Higher Education, *The Fourth Revolution.*

[40] "Library Education and Manpower; A Statement of Policy Adopted by the Council of the American Library Association, June 30, 1970" (Chicago: American Library Association, 1970). (Mimeographed.)

[41] American Association of School Librarians. School Library Manpower Project, *School Library Personnel Task Analysis Survey*. Prepared by the Research Division, National Education Association (Chicago: American Library Association, 1969).

[42] American Association of School Librarians. School Library Manpower Project, *Occupational Definitions for School Library Media Personnel*.

[43] Wallington and others, *Jobs in Instructional Media*.

[44] *North American Library Education*, pp. 30-31.

[45] T. M. Stinnett, *A Manual on Certification Requirements for School Personnel in the United States* (1970 ed.; Washington: National Education Association, 1970).

[46] Robert N. Case, "Experimental Models for School Library Media Education," *School Library Journal*, XVIII (December 1971), 25-30.

[47] Carnegie Commission on Higher Education, *The Fourth Revolution*.

[48] Seven of the models are described in "Teacher Education Models," *Journal of Research and Development in Education* (University of Georgia), II, No. 3 (Spring 1969). The full reports of these model programs, published by the Government Printing Office in 1968, are listed in the Appendix to this paper (see pp. 51-52).

[49] Jesse H. Shera, "Research Needs Relating to the Aims and Content of Graduate Library Education," in *A Study of the Needs for Research in Library and Information Science Education; Final Report*. Harold Borko (Los Angeles: University of California, Institute of Library Research, October 31, 1970), p. 22.

[50] Margaret Hayes Grazier, "Preparation of the School Librarian," in *Education for Librarianship; The Design of the Curriculum of Library Schools*, ed. by Herbert Goldhor (Urbana: University of Illinois, 1971), p. 139.

[51] Harry S. Broudy, "A Critique of Performance-Based Teacher Education" (Washington: American Association of Colleges for Teacher Education, May 1972).

[52] "Standards and Guidelines for the Approval of Institutions and Programs for Teacher Education: Competency-Based Programs" (Raleigh, N.C.: State Department of Public Instruction, May 30, 1972). (Mimeographed.)

[53] Case, "Experimental Models for School Library Media Education"; and Anna Mary Lowrey, "Components of Curriculum Innovation," *Journal of Education for Librarianship*, XII (Spring 1972), 247-53.

BIBLIOGRAPHY

American Association of School Librarians. *Standards for School Library Programs*. Chicago: American Library Association, 1960.

American Association of School Librarians. School Library Manpower Project. *Occupational Definitions for School Library Media Personnel*. Chicago: American Library Association, 1971.

——————— . *School Library Personnel Task Analysis Survey*. Prepared by the

Research Division, National Education Association. Chicago: American Library Association, 1969.

American Association of School Librarians and Department of Audiovisual Instruction. *Standards for School Media Programs.* Chicago: American Library Association; Washington: National Education Association, 1969.

American Library Association. Committee on Post-War Planning. *School Libraries for Today and Tomorrow: Functions and Standards.* Chicago: American Library Association, 1945.

Asheim, Lester E. "Education and Manpower for Librarianship: First Steps Toward a Statement of Policy." *ALA Bulletin,* LXII (October 1968), 1096-1106.

Atkins, Neil P. "Introduction." *Curricular Concerns in a Revolutionary Era.* Ed. by Robert R. Leeper. Washington: Association for Supervision and Curriculum Development, 1971.

Audiovisual Instruction, XIV (January 1969).

Brickell, Henry M. "Implementing Educational Change." *School Libraries,* XIX (Summer 1970), 17-23.

Broudy, Harry S. "A Critique of Performance-Based Teacher Education." Washington: American Association of Colleges for Teacher Education, May 1972.

Burton, Phillip. "Education Tomorrow." *The Futurist,* III (December 1969), 150.

Carnegie Commission on Higher Education. *The Fourth Revolution; Instructional Technology in Higher Education.* New York: McGraw-Hill, 1972.

Case, Robert N. "Experimental Models for School Library Media Education." *School Library Journal,* XVIII (December 1971), 25-30.

Commission on Instructional Technology. *To Improve Learning; An Evaluation of Instructional Technology.* Sidney G. Tickton, ed. 2 vols. New York: Bowker, 1970.

Davies, Ruth Ann. *The School Library: A Force for Educational Excellence.* New York: Bowker, 1970.

Educational Policies Commission. *The Central Purpose of American Education.* Washington: National Education Association, 1961.

"Encouraging Instruction in the Use of Instructional Materials." Washington: Association for Supervision and Curriculum Development, 1958. (Mimeographed.)

Gaver, Mary V. *Services of Secondary School Media Centers: Evaluation and Development.* Chicago: American Library Association, 1971.

Geller, Evelyn. "So Near and Yet So Far: Libraries and Open Schools." *School Library Journal,* XVIII (February 1972), 40-44.

Graham, Mae, ed. "The Changing Nature of the School Library." *Library Trends,* XVII (April 1969), 343-433.

Grazier, Margaret Hayes. "The High School Library in Transition." Chicago: American Association of School Librarians, Knapp School Libraries Project, 1967. (Mimeographed.)

——————— . "The Library and New Programs." *The Bulletin of the National Association of Secondary-School Principals,* L (January 1966), 18-24.

——————— . "Preparation of the School Librarian." *Education for Librarian-*

ship; The Design of the Curriculum of Library Schools. Ed. by Herbert Goldhor. Urbana: University of Illinois, 1971.

Harlow, Neal. "Commentary." *Student Use of Libraries; An Inquiry into the Needs of Students, Libraries, and the Educational Process*. Chicago: American Library Association, 1964.

Henne, Frances. "Learning to Learn in School Libraries." *School Libraries*, XV (May 1966), 15-17.

————— . "The Challenge of Change—New Standards for New Times." *Bulletin of the National Association of Secondary-School Principals*, L (January 1966), 75-81.

Herman, Gertrude. "The Open Corridor Schools and the Library." *School Library Journal*, XIX (September 1972), 36-40.

Kohl, Herbert. *The Open Classroom*. New York: Random House, 1970.

"Library Education and Manpower; A Statement of Policy Adopted by the Council of the American Library Association, June 30, 1970." Chicago: American Library Association, 1970. (Mimeographed.)

Lowrey, Anna Mary. "Components of Curriculum Innovation." *Journal of Education for Librarianship*, XII (Spring 1972), 247-53.

National Education Association. Center for the Study of Instruction. *Schools for the 70's and Beyond: A Call to Action*. Washington: National Education Association, 1971.

National Education Association. Department of Audiovisual Instruction. *Quantitative Standards for Audiovisual Personnel, Equipment and Materials in Elementary, Secondary, and Higher Education*. Washington: the Department, 1966. (Mimeographed.)

National Education Association. Project on the Instructional Program of the Public Schools. *Deciding What to Teach*. Washington: National Education Association, 1963.

National American Library Education; Directory and Statistics, 1969-1971. Frank L. Schick and D. Kathryn Weintraub, eds. Chicago: American Library Association, 1972.

Rowell, John, and M. Ann Heidbreder. *Educational Media Selection Centers: Identification and Analysis of Current Practices*. Chicago: American Library Association, 1971.

Saddler, Virginia B. "Role of the Library in Education." Unpublished manuscript, Barbourville, Kentucky, 1970.

Sand, Ole. *On Staying Awake: Talks with Teachers*. Washington: National Education Association, Center for the Study of Instruction, 1970.

Shera, Jesse H. "Research Needs Relating to the Aims and Content of Graduate Library Education." *A Study of the Needs for Research in Library and Information Science Education*. Final Report. Harold Borko. Los Angeles: University of California, Institute of Library Research, October 31, 1970.

————— . "Staffing Library Services to Meet Student Needs—Library Education." *Student Use of Libraries; An Inquiry into the Needs of Students, Libraries, and the Educational Process*. Chicago: American Library Association, 1964.

Silberman, Charles E. *Crisis in the Classroom; The Remaking of American Education*. New York: Random House, 1970.

"Standards and Guidelines for the Approval of Institutions and Programs for Teacher Education: Competency-Based Programs." Raleigh, N.C.: State Department of Public Instruction, May 30, 1972. (Mimeographed.)

Stinnett, T. M. *A Manual on Certification Requirements for School Personnel in the United States.* 1970 ed. Washington: National Education Association, 1970.

"Teacher Education Models." *Journal of Research and Development in Education* (University of Georgia), II, No. 3 (Spring 1969).

"To Promote Competency of Use of Library Resources." Chicago: American Association of School Librarians, 1960. (Mimeographed.)

Van Orden, Phyllis Jeanne. "Use of Media and the Media Center, as Reflected in Professional Journals for Elementary School Teachers." Unpublished Ed.D. dissertation, Wayne State University, 1970.

Walker, Jerry L. "What Do Student Teachers Know about Libraries?" *School Libraries*, XVI (Winter 1967), 17-18, 23.

Wallington, C. James, and others, eds. *Jobs in Instructional Media.* Washington: Association for Educational Communications and Technology, 1970.

Witt, Paul W.F. "Preservice Education of Teachers in the Selection and Use of All Types of Instructional Materials with Implications for the Library." *The School Library as a Materials Center.* Ed. by Mary Helen Mahar. Washington: U.S. Department of Health, Education, and Welfare, Office of Education, 1964.

——————. "Teacher Education and School Libraries." *School Libraries*, XIV (October 1964), 37-46.

APPENDIX

NINE TEACHER EDUCATION MODELS
BUREAU OF RESEARCH, U.S. OFFICE OF EDUCATION

Florida State University. *A Model for the Preparation of Elementary School Teachers.* Washington: Government Printing Office, 1968.

Michigan State University. *Behavioral Science Elementary Teacher Education Program.* Washington: Government Printing Office, 1968. Vols. I-III.

Northwest Regional Educational Laboratory. *A Competency Based, Field Centered, Systems Approach to Elementary Teacher Education.* Washington: Government Printing Office, 1968.

Syracuse University. *Specifications for a Comprehensive Undergraduate and Inservice Teacher Education Program for Elementary Teachers.* Washington: Government Printing Office, 1968.

Teachers College, Columbia University. *The Teacher-Innovator: A Program to Prepare Teachers.* Washington: Government Printing Office, 1968.

University of Georgia. *Georgia Educational Model Specifications for the Preparation of Elementary Teachers.* Washington: Government Printing Office, 1968.

University of Massachusetts. *Model Elementary Teacher Education Program.* Washington: Government Printing Office, 1968.

University of Pittsburgh. *A Model of Teacher Training for the Individualization of Instruction.* Washington: Government Printing Office, 1968.

University of Toledo. *Education Specifications for a Comprehensive Elementary Teacher Education Program.* Washington: Government Printing Office, 1968. Vols. I-III.

LIBRARY EDUCATION FOR THE FUTURE: THE COLLEGE AND UNIVERSITY LIBRARY

Stanley McElderry

Director
The University of Chicago Library

The recent history of higher education in the United States has demonstrated clearly that the character and function of the academic library is closely related to changes taking place within colleges and universities. The kinds of competencies required to manage these libraries is likewise related to the emerging role of the academic library and the kinds of technology which are available.

Higher education enjoyed unparalleled prosperity in the decade of the sixties. Enrollments increased from three million students to well over six million. The college population was more diversified as larger numbers of low-income and minority groups entered higher education. At the same time larger numbers of students continued on into graduate education, and the number of doctoral degrees awarded more than tripled. New fields (such as area studies, urban studies, ethnic studies, ecology, etc.) were introduced in the curriculum in response to demands. Further expansion in research was reflected in increased governmental support and the creation of research institutes to foster interdisciplinary approaches to problems. The quality of university research activity was generally acknowledged to be the best in the world, and faculties were contributing their services to the resolution of problems in both the public and private sectors of society.

The rapid expansion of higher education and its attendant costs accelerated by inflation led to financial crises. Economic recession and a loss of public confidence in higher education, attributed to widespread student protest, restricted the capacity and willingness of the public to maintain support for higher education. The Carnegie Commission on Higher Education, established in 1969 to assess the current situation, characterized it as:

> . . . a period of the deepest trouble ever experienced by higher education in this country. The past three to four years has seen unprecedented unrest and disorder on the campus, a loss of public confidence in higher education, reduction of financial support for it, and a crisis in the financial viability of at least a third of our colleges and universities. . . .[1]

Academic libraries shared in the prosperity of the sixties and in the current financial crises. Collections increased at an unprecedented rate and were enlarged in scope as new programs and activities were added to colleges and universities. Staff increased rapidly during this period to process new acquisitions and to provide new services. More emphasis was placed on special competencies such as foreign languages, advanced subject specialties, and managerial skills as the library organization became large and complex. Libraries began to introduce technological innovations, like the computer, to augment services and to control rising costs. These efforts have not been sufficient to withstand the financial pressures on academic administrators, for library budgets are now being cut or, at best, remain at the same level. Staff lay-offs are not uncommon as services are pruned, collection development is curtailed, and further economies are being explored.

Higher education is currently experiencing the most intensive analysis and appraisal in its history. The literature is filled with proposals for reform and with uncertain predictions for the future of higher education. At the same time librarians are reminded that current techniques for the collection, organization, and dissemination of information are costly, inefficient, and on the verge of collapse under the weight of the increasing volume of publishing and the growing demands for information. Technological innovations are being advanced by some proponents as the means for revolutionizing the educational process and radically changing the role of libraries. At this time of reassessment, reflection, and speculation about the future, it is important to know the direction of change in the future, its probable impact on libraries, and how we can prepare for these changes.

In describing a program for the preparation of academic librarians in the future we must first examine probable trends in higher education itself and their impact on academic libraries. Secondly we must explore the relationships of technological advances as they may influence library operation. After we have identified the probable role of the library from assessment of these trends, we may gain a better understanding of the competencies required for academic librarians in the future.

Higher Education

The factors in higher education which have been most closely associated with changes in the library are the demands for higher education, the composition of the student body, the nature and emphasis of the curriculum, the instructional methods employed, and the services and activities performed by the faculty.

It is anticipated that enrollment in higher education will continue to grow in the period of the seventies and then level off after 1980. The U.S. Office of Education predicts a 50 percent increase in enrollment by 1980 at which point demand will remain relatively constant.[2] If these predictions hold true there will be a student population of ten million in 1980 compared to three million in 1960 and seven million at present.

There are a number of factors beyond demographic data which may influence the size and growth rate of college populations and alter the present

54

mix of students. Ted R. Vaughan and Gideon Sjoberg[3] believe that the change in the labor force from one dominated by manufacturing to one where the service sector is in the majority will increase demands for higher education. This change could increase social pressures for professionalization of many occupations in the service sector. It is further asserted that as governmental agencies assume a larger role in providing social services, bureaucracies on the federal, state, and local levels will grow and further specialization may result. Changes in priorities may produce increased emphasis on health care and on study of environmental issues.

The transition to the post-industrial society is expected to result in technological unemployment for many persons and to require retraining for new positions. The accelerated pace of discovery and generation of new knowledge will require further retraining or continued training for many specialized occupations. Increased leisure time resulting from automation, reduction of the work week, and earlier retirement are perceived as a further stimulus to educational opportunity.

Advanced education has been a major factor in social mobility in the past and is viewed as a major element in producing greater egalitarianism for ethnic minorities, women, and socially disadvantaged persons.

The expanded role which higher education may have to play in the future is expected to increase the number of persons beyond the normal college age attending colleges and universities. There may also be a broader representation of students from different socio-economic background and ethnic groups than there has been in the past.

Increased variety in the composition of the student population is expected to generate demands for new programs to meet the needs and interests of a more heterogeneous student body. It may be necessary to introduce more remedial programs to compensate for deficiencies in educational background. More vocationally-oriented programs will almost certainly be required in retraining those technologically unemployed or in updating the knowledge of persons in highly specialized fields.

There is more uncertainty in the area of graduate education, since the demand for Ph.D.'s is increasing and research activity appears to be slackening. Outside support for research has been reduced but is anticipated to continue on a more modest level. Changing priorities may provide greater opportunities for research and service in areas such as environmental protection, renovation of urban life and improved health care, and other fields of social interest.

Much of the recent student criticism (about higher education) relates to instructional methods, and it is not surprising that most campuses have engaged in reexamination of their programs. The American Association of University Professors has given considerable attention to the instructional process. Their conclusion is that the vast majority of faculty are concerned about instruction but that the college environments are not as supportive of teaching as they could be. A recent study concludes:

> ... the widespread concern for undergraduate teaching on the part of students, administrators, and the public is shared by large numbers of faculty members. If the call to improve the quality of teaching is to be

heeded, innovative ideas and new departures from traditional academic policies and practices are necessary. Institutional policies which clearly support teaching as well as procedures to utilize the contributions of students and colleagues hold promise for enhancing traditional teaching environments. Several colleges and universities are creating alternative teaching and learning environments which transcend the limitations of such traditional concepts as a self-centered campus, a curriculum isolated from the rest of student life, a fragmented disciplinary approach to teaching, a standardized course, and a single program. Such innovative contexts alongside traditional settings may allow higher education to provide a variety of environments which will meet the diverse needs of students, teachers, and society.[4]

Improvement of the instructional process is expected to occur through two approaches. The first is a more conscious analysis of what should be taught and how to teach it. The second approach is a systematic assessment of alternative methods, including technological devices, for achieving more carefully defined objectives. The emerging field of educational design and technology is expected to provide guidance and assistance in this process. This is a complex area and no major breakthroughs are anticipated in the immediate future. A period of innovation and systematic appraisal bringing increased costs initially will precede wider application. New technology is regarded as a supplement to classroom instruction, a substitute for instruction in certain skill areas, and an aid to off-campus instruction. The library could potentially benefit as the host for self-instructional devices.[5]

The Carnegie Commission on Higher Education has sponsored a variety of studies pointing up the opportunities available to higher education and recommending various courses of action. They view the role of the federal government as vital in correcting current inadequacies and in exploiting the potential of higher education. They state:

> In the past, through initiative expressed in the form of aid, the federal government moved our colleges and universities to make substantial advances in agriculture and in scientific research and graduate education; now with selective support, the federal government can use its initiative to increase equality of educational opportunity, expand the supply of health manpower, and encourage desirable innovation and reform.
>
> Selective aid at the federal level has been, and can be, a major force for drawing higher education into high-priority social endeavors.[6]

Trends in Libraries and Information Services

It is instructive to assess the future role of the academic library, as it may be modified through technology, in the broad context of information transfer. A number of devices have been proposed which could radically change library procedures and challenge the institutional framework within which the library operates. It may be anticipated, therefore, that with renewed support, the demand for higher education will continue to increase, that it may assume new functions as it responds to the needs of society, and that new approaches may be introduced to revitalize the teaching process.

The impact of trends in higher education on academic libraries in the future will be continued enrollment expansion in some institutions but with a more highly diversified population. Changing priorities in society and changes in the labor market will produce new areas for collection development and de-emphasis in others. Although the emphasis on research will remain strong, new services may be required to serve a heterogeneous population and to exploit educational technology. The library's role as a center for independent study may be expanded as the function of the classroom is more critically defined and more programmed materials employing a wider range of technological devices become available.

A number of basic processes may be identified in the generation and dissemination of information as it is related to libraries. In block diagram they may be identified as follows:

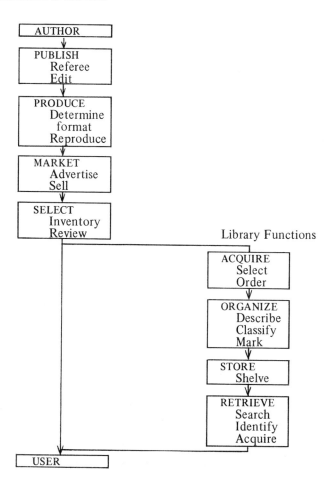

It may be observed that there are many discrete steps in the generation and dissemination of information. Initially the process is begun by negotiations between the author and the publisher. The latter function is performed by a wide variety of organizations with different standards, specialties, and motivations for disseminating information. The function is highly structured with thousands of organizations involved on a world-wide basis, but a few organizations control a large part of the total volume. The production phase is often related to the publishing process but may be quite independent. Important decisions regarding composition and format may be made at this stage affecting the utility, cost, and availability of publications. The marketing phase may be viewed as a wholesale function closely integrated to publishing and production, but it may also be viewed as a retail operation serving a number of publishers as a book jobber. The economic motive may be strong at this stage with respect to acquiring and keeping the item available for acquisition. There are thousands of businesses engaged in the marketing operation and they vary significantly in their utility as a source of supply. The selection phase is defined in a special sense to identify a series of operations that may be performed to make an item more readily known. There is a national inventory step which lists an item among the majority of other newly published works. It varies in scope among developed countries but is generally quite comprehensive. A related step is the review or appraisal of the work in reviewing media. Only a fraction of new publications are referred in this manner and the quality of reviewing is very uneven. Sometimes a work is reviewed in several sources but only the most popular receive such jury treatment. There are few conventions followed in this process, hence the utility of the review may be limited.

The traditional library functions assume a retail function for the user and include the processes of acquisition, organization, storage, and retrieval. The library has been the only organization which has systematically carried on these functions. Libraries tend to be identified by the clientele they serve and the activities the users are engaged in. The academic library, for example, serves the instructional and research activities of the academic community which support it. The responsibilities it assumes, therefore, may be quite broad or narrowly circumscribed.

The library selects from the world of publishing those works which it can identify as relating to the needs of its clientele. Since the quantity of items current and retrospective is vast, the library relies on many devices for selection. Works can rarely be appraised directly so reviews are scanned, bibliographies examined, and a variety of other criteria employed such as the reputation of the author or publisher, the apparent appropriateness of the title, its format, language, etc. The selection process is time-consuming and is dominated by many subjective factors. The larger the budget and the more extensive the program commitment of the institution is, the more hospitable it is to selection of marginal items. It is suspected that libraries acquire numerous titles so that the scholarly community can perform the evaluation function which is inadequately carried out at an earlier stage.

The ordering function of a large academic library is a tedious, time-consuming operation. There are numerous sources of supply and only a few jobbers who can supply the more popular items. Many titles must be acquired from source, and these sources vary enormously in promptness and efficiency.

Following the receipt of an item in the library, the organization processes begin. These involve standard identification of the title following conventional practices, designation of subjects and other characteristics of significance for retrieval, such as joint authors, series, etc., assignment of a location number (generally by its major subject), and affixing appropriate ownership marks. The more intellectual aspects of this operation may be performed by national sources, such as the Library of Congress, leaving only a more routine editing function to the individual library. In smaller libraries much of this function may be subcontracted to a jobber who supplies a shelf-ready book on direction.

The storage process seems commonplace, but it is influenced by many decisions made earlier in the information transfer process. The format of the item or the manner in which it is packaged has considerable significance on the mode of storage and the efficiency of its retrieval. If it is in microprint or issued in a published series it cannot easily be integrated with other materials on the same subject. The variety of formats has reached the points where there is no longer an integrated body of information in a physical sense. Rather, the library collection consists of a variety of discrete bodies of information, physically separated, and with unique retrieval devices.

The retrieval process is the most complex activity in the library, for it attempts to relate the needs of the user to specific publications which satisfy his requirements. This activity is supported by the card catalog—a unique local finding device—and a wide variety of bibliographies, indexes, and finding tools. The more commonplace lists of information may be extracted from source and organized in reference works such as encyclopedias, dictionaries, handbooks, etc. The sources available to support retrieval are so voluminous that considerable knowledge, experience, and sophistication are required to perform a search procedure. The rapid growth of collections and the appearance of new formats has added complexity and confusion to the process. There is little, if any, standardization of search strategies, and there is no conceptual base for the data elements used in the process.

This review of the information transfer process as it relates to the library reveals many deficiencies in the process and identifies complexities in the adoption of new technology. It is evident that there are numerous individuals and organizations involved in generating and disseminating information. There is little coordination between the steps in the process, and much inefficiency results. The generating and dissemination system is not designed for efficiency at the retrieval end, hence a library is forced to adapt to the process as it is currently operating. As the volume of new publications is increased and the residual store increases in mass, it is obvious that costs are rising rapidly and the relative efficiency of a conventional library decreases. Many libraries have doubled in size in the last decade and inflation has doubled the price of books and, in some instances, quadrupled the cost of staff.

Much of the new technology relating to libraries is concerned with computers to mechanize record functions and accelerate retrieval functions, to store information in a uniform format such as microfiche, which will reduce space and permit mechanization of storage and retrieval functions, and to electronic transmission of information either bibliographic, textual, or both. In concept it is easy to see how the current library procedures might be simplified, and it is clear that a large corporation or governmental agency could implement many of these proposals because they can control and coordinate all the steps in the process of information transfer. Under such circumstances it is possible to identify more clearly the retrieval requirements and design the support system. It is not clear at the present stage of technological development whether the program would be economically feasible, and there are vast deficiencies in our understanding of how people learn and of what is involved in the research process. Consequently, we are not readily able to state the specifications for an efficient information retrieval system.

Evaluating the traditional library as a part of the information transfer process provides useful insight into the library's current deficiencies and the utility of future technology. It identifies as variables the nature and format of conventional collections and the modes of organizing and providing access to them. It raises questions about the viability of local bases of funding and control and the interrelationship of libraries. There are further questions concerning the dependence of users upon the knowledge and experience of the librarian in the retrieval process.

It is not anticipated that the function of the academic library will change radically in the immediate future. Its primary function is to support the instructional and research programs of its parent institution. These programs are subject to change as the needs of its population change and as national priorities and funding sources may influence research endeavors. The impact of these changes is reflected primarily in collection building. The academic library has a potential role in supplementing the instructional program and in providing avenues for independent study. The extent to which these functions are assumed varies with the financial ability of the institution and its educational philosophy. The potential of the library for self-study and as an avenue for life-long learning is not fully exploited or consciously supported. It should receive increased emphasis in the future as the function of the classroom is better defined.

The relationships between academic and research libraries as well as other types of libraries may change as we move toward open access to information. Currently we lack the definition of what information needs are and the mechanisms required to provide better coordination among libraries. We lack the specific information on resources held by libraries to plan efficient access to information. The ability to share resources is further limited by time constraints imposed by course demands and research deadlines. The area of greatest potential cooperation in the immediate future is in the joint acquisition of little-used materials.

Academic libraries need to recognize the potential impact of new technology on the format of collections and on access devices and the opportunities which may be afforded for coordination in planning access to information through new institutional relationships. It is not anticipated, however, that new technology will be introduced in a revolutionay manner. A period of analysis and experimentation is needed before the appropriate direction in the future may be determined. Following this step there will be efforts to adopt standards on a broad national and international basis and to seek coordinated approaches to implementation.

Training for Academic Librarians

The analysis of trends in higher education and in technological devices for handling information sources indicates that academic libraries may be called upon to play an expanded role in the instructional process and in the support of research endeavor. The areas of interest may shift as colleges and universities respond to changes in society. Service requirements may be altered as a more diversified population seeks support for their informational needs. Changes in the instructional process and the use of programmed materials may result in more direct responsibility for the library in the conduct of independent study programs. Developments in technology in the educational and information fields could have a profound effect on higher education and the role of the library in this process. These trends will undoubtedly require new insights and new competencies in managing academic libraries in the future.

In reflecting upon the training of college and university librarians in the future, it is desirable to assess the current status of library education and some of the anticipated changes. The preparation of academic librarians is an integral part of the training of all librarians, and an understanding of common elements may be helpful in identification of unique competencies required in the academic field. In assessing library education we shall examine the process by which the content of the curriculum is defined, comment on instructional methods in the light of current educational thinking, and comment on the relationship of the school in its institutional setting and in its status in the profession. More specific recommendations on the training of academic librarians will be made in the light of this assessment.

Much of our reasoning about the definition of a program of studies for the preparation of persons for librarianship stems from the characteristics of professional work. Without laboring the question of whether librarianship is a profession, we can identify characteristics of professions which are useful in understanding the relationship of librarianship to other occupations and to society generally. Among these characteristics are a commitment to the service of others by the application of esoteric knowledge and techniques which are learned through prolonged study and experience and the relative autonomy of the practitioner in "the creative handling of novelty," to use Hiltner's phrase, in the service of others. The body of knowledge is systematically extended through the discovery of new insights relating to opportunities for service and new techniques for ministering to needs. Hiltner distinguished between professional and vocational education in these terms:

> A profession is different because of the demands it puts on adaptability to new and unique problems and situations. Professional education, therefore, must be education in principles which have wide range of application. Professional education is supposed to produce insight; vocational training is content to produce repetitive knacks and automatic skills . . . exploration, research, discovery or rediscovery are inherent in professional education.[7]

If we assume that these characteristics of a profession have relevance for librarianship, the problem of a library educator is to identify the body of knowledge and principles which are required for the practitioner. There are several approaches which may be used to resolve this question. We might ask the leading practitioners to identify the information needed for successful practice, but this tends to be subjective, and it is difficult to reach a consensus. Opinions will also vary with the nature of the experience of the practitioners and will change over time. Another approach is to analyze the activities of librarians in detail through job analysis and attempt to identify the knowledge required to perform various skills. This approach was used by librarianship at an earlier time, but the definition of requisite skills tends to change and is often quite superficial. Another method might be simply to avoid definition and attempt to expose prospective librarians to the "best" minds and most successful library practitioners. There would tend to be no organization to the curriculum, overemphasis in some areas and neglect in others, and a highly unstable program over time.

Most of the approaches described above have been utilized by library educators at one time or another and have probably led to much of the current emphasis on vocational skills as opposed to a more theoretical orientation. Library schools have tended to respond to the immediate needs of libraries as they exist today, and this introduces a basic conflict between practitioners and library educators. Many libraries today are inadequate in resources and provide only marginal service. Librarians are conservative and are reluctant to give up established practices even though they may be inefficient and often wasteful. The curriculum cannot be determined solely by current practices because it will not produce people who can respond to changing needs or take advantage of new opportunities and techniques. Such a program would also tend to drive away potential librarians with abilities which might lead to constructive change.

Library education must start, therefore, with a clearer insight into the societal processes in which it participates. Library services should not be defined simply by tradition, but through identification of services that libraries can render. This process leads to the definition of the library of the future. In a sense all practitioners attempt to do this by analysis of the population served, the characteristics of users and non-users, and the factors which lead to greater utilization of library resources. What is suggested here, however, is to examine more closely the activities of the population to gain further insight into how people learn and how and what kinds of information sources facilitate the process. We need to know how discoveries are made and what takes place in research activity in identification of a problem for investigation and in the chain of events which takes place in its resolution. We need a better understanding of the kinds of decisions people make and the sources of information which would assist them. Considerable study has been made of the learning process, the philosophy and sociology of knowledge, and decision making by persons in other disciplines, but very little of it is reflected in the current library school curriculum.

An essential ingredient in professional education, therefore, is an understanding of what services it can render to society now and in the future. All service-oriented enterprises have the same problem if they are to survive. They must have a clear insight into what the public needs and will buy, and they must continue to adapt their services and products to meet changing circumstances.

From the earlier analysis of the information transfer process we can identify a number of unique functions which libraries have traditionally performed. These are: building collections of information to serve varying information needs, organizing collections for efficient access, and providing guidance and instruction in securing information. It is apparent that the techniques by which these functions have been performed are subject to radical change with the application of new technology. The format of information is variable, the composition and physical location of collections is subject to redefinition, modes of access may change through the use of computers and electronic transmission, and the relative dependence of the client on the practitioner may be altered. The only thing we can be reasonably sure of is that people will continue to have information needs and that the nature of their activities will tend to increase the requirements for information. We cannot, therefore, proceed from a statement of library objectives to a definition of what functions libraries should perform. The functions are inherent in the information transfer process. What responsibilities the library assumes and the methods that are employed are variable and are subject to continuous refinement and change.

In designing a curriculum for a library school, it is necessary to be aware of current market requirements so that a graduate from the program can function effectively in libraries as they now exist. At the very least, however, he should understand current "best" practices as well as they can be defined, the basic problems being addressed by these practices, the limitations of current approaches, the information needed to improve these practices, and how to secure or identify reliable information relevant to the improvement of current practices. One would hope that such understanding would be tolerant of current approaches and systematic and objective in seeking new solutions.

In trying to deal with the problem of current as well as future curricula for librarians it is necessary to phrase specifications in terms of general competencies rather than specific types of courses. The structure of the curriculum is implicit in much of the previous discussion. It would consist of the following elements:

1. *The purpose and function of libraries and/or information services*

This is not a new label for "The Libraries in Society" type of course but an attempt to understand the intellectual and communication processes which require access to information. The focus is on the activity, not on the physical, social, ethnic, and economic status of the clientele. The objective is to acquire perspective on what libraries are and can be through whatever sources will yield a meaningful insight. We have traditionally attempted this by courses in the history of libraries and scholarship, reading studies, the library as a medium of communication, or now the library as an information transfer mechanism. All of these approaches have been useful, but there are other disciplines—such as learning theory, the philosophy of science, the sociology of knowledge, etc.—which could be selectively useful for various types of libraries. This area as currently presented is frequently superficial and appears irrelevant to the student. However, as previously indicated, this is the area which gives meaning and direction to the profession.

2. *Building collections of informational sources*

As previously stated, the format of information and how it is packaged may change radically over time, but it is believed that the need to perform this function systematically and with increasing precision for various users will continue to be a prime function.

3. *Organizing collections of informational sources for efficient access*

This area encompasses what we have traditionally labeled cataloging and classification, but the attempt here is to view the function in the broad context and to encompass new technologies. It could be projected beyond current cataloging and classification techniques to analysis of data elements and evaluation devices relating to more efficient retrieval of information for selective purposes.

4. *Interpretation of informational sources*

The present courses in reference and bibliography are typically included in this area. They tend to focus primarily upon the tools rather than the client. Although this relationship is understood, we have not systematically related user problems to the development of specifications for reference tools or data elements required for effective evaluation of information for specific purposes.

5. *Application of basic functions to a type of clientele*

There is some question whether types of library courses fulfill this function, but it would appear that the requirements of various clientele and the approaches employed to meet their needs are sufficiently different to require courses in this area. The inclusion of this area permits identification of the general problems common to types of libraries and demonstration of how basic functions are adapted to a particular situation.

6. *Tool skills*

Sophistication in research methodology would appear to be essential for utilizing information and resolving problems. There are a wide range of skills now applicable to libraries, skills such as statistics systems analysis, cost accounting, cumputer programming, etc. These skills will be increasingly important in the future.

The six areas identified above might be viewed as a core applicable to all prospective librarians, but there are obviously some types of information which would be more useful for one type of library. The areas have been addressed more specifically to the academic library field, but they are sufficiently broad to encompass additional specialization and more than one course. Further specialization in subject areas, in tool subjects, or in functions such as management would seem more appropriate for interdisciplinary cooperation than a superficial course in the library school. This would seem particularly necessary for post-master's study, where the librarian should have as much sophistication in his outside specialty as graduate students in the same discipline.

This analysis does not prescribe specific admission requirements to the program because it is assumed that librarianship will become increasingly specialized and some traditional functions in areas such as the technical services may not be performed in every library. It may not be desirable, therefore, to specify competencies which should be common to all students, e.g., languages, mathematics, computer programming, etc.

There are a number of other general criticisms of higher education which must be considered in the reappraisal of library education. Educators are not in complete agreement on what education is, and the tendency is to emphasize content. Many educators now view education as the cultivation of problem-solving skills with less emphasis on specific content and a stronger focus on problem identification, analysis, and information gathering. The process is viewed further as continuous and life-long with an eternal quest for meaning and relevance.

Library educators will need to decide upon the appropriate emphasis on content and skills, and it is anticipated that greater attention will be given to a more explicit definition of what should be taught and a systematic assessment of alternative approaches. The methodology and discipline of instructional design and technology may provide assistance in this process, but it will not be applied without the investment of the time and money required to discover and to apply new approaches effectively.

A common criticism of library education is its isolation from other disciplines and from the professional generally. To the extent that the situation obtains, it must be countered vigorously, for the rate of change is accelerating and there is concern that the current curriculum is not relevant to current practice in the profession. Interdisciplinary approaches are being employed to establish closer relationships with allied disciplines. Closer contacts with libraries would be helpful in understanding current problems and the approaches being used to help resolve them. Such contacts would also be useful in motivating the student by relating training to first-hand experience. The problem of isolation is generally appreciated, but most library schools do not have the liberal funding that other disciplines enjoy to provide opportunities for faculty to maintain contacts with leading practitioners in the profession and to observe current practices first-hand. It is apparent further that library school faculties rarely lead the profession in research and experimentation as is frequently true of other professions. A stronger research orientation and closer relationship to current practice is needed to restore balance in library education.

Much of the foregoing discussion of library education relates to the general program and its orientation. Most of the requirements for preparation of academic libraries appear to be subsumed in the proposed training for all librarians. The specific needs in the academic area relate to the nature of the clientele served and to the intellectual activities in which they are engaged. These appear to be sufficiently complex that they require special attention. It also seems desirable to consider special problems in the field and current approaches to these problems. These requirements would be common to any library serving a clientle with similar orientation, but they are more readily identifiable in academic institutions. It is assumed that there will be opportunities in a training program for increased specialization in subject fields, language skills, and other managerial skills. It is not anticipated that such areas of specialization would be common to all students.

In summary, the kinds of competencies required to manage academic libraries in the future are closely associated with changes occurring within higher education and information technology. Higher education is expected to have a new and expanded role to play in response to changes in the structure of the labor force and changing national priorities. These changes are expected to change the composition of the student body with respect to age distribution, sex, and ethnic and disadvantaged groups. The new mix of the student population will manifest itself in different areas of interest and different emphases that may now exist. Research activity will continue to play a major role on university campuses. The reexamination of instructional methods and the adoption of new analytical techniques will refine the instructional process and lead to the introduction of a wide range of approaches. Technological devices employing new formats and representational dimensions will be used selectively to supplement and augment classroom instruction. The computer and new devices for electronic transmission will be applied to aid instruction and extend the geographic limits of access. The analytical methods required for evaluation of current methods and assessment of new approaches may be as important in refining education methods as new technology itself.

The academic librarian of the future will need to understand the implication of changes in higher education and the opportunities afforded by new technology. He will need more sophisticated understanding of the clientele served, particularly the intellectual activities they are engaged in, and of the traditional functions of the library in the information transfer process. The potential changes in format of information and in modes of storage and access will be required. The appropriate adaptation of processes to activities of clientle will require understanding and skill in the use of at least some of the new tools for analysis and measurement. Some additional specialization in either subject fields, language or management will be essential.

FOOTNOTES

[1] The Carnegie Commission on Higher Education, *An Interim Report by the President of the Carnegie Foundation for the Advancement of Teaching* (the Commission, 1971), p. 4.

[2] The Carnegie Commission on Higher Education, *The More Effective Use of Resources: An Imperative for Higher Education* (New York: McGraw-Hill, 1972), p. 7.

[3] Ted R. Vaughan and Gideon Sjoberg, "The Politics of Projection: A Critique of Cartter's Analysis," *Science*, CLXXVII, No. 4044 (July 14, 1972), 42.

[4] Jerry G. Goff and Robert C. Wilson, "The Teaching Environment," *AAUP Bulletin*, LVII, No. 4 (December 1971), 493.

[5] The Carnegie Commission on Higher Education. *The Fourth Revolution; Instructional Technology in Higher Education* (New York: McGraw-Hill, 1972), pp. 4-5.

[6] *The Chronicle of Higher Education*, VI, No. 12 (December 13, 1971), 14.

[7] Seward Hiltner, "The Essentials of Professional Education," *Journal of Higher Education*, XXV (May 1954), 250.

APPENDIX
PROPOSED CURRICULUM
FOR COLLEGE AND UNIVERSITY LIBRARIANS

Core for All Librarians	Selected Examples of Additional Requirements for Academic Librarians
	1 additional course from this area:
Purpose and Function of Libraries	Higher Education
	Learning Theory
	Philosophy of Science
	1 area from the following for specialization:
Building Collections of Informational Materials	Advanced Bibliography
Organizing Collections	Advanced Cataloging
	Indexing and Abstracting
Interpretation of Information Sources	Subject Reference Sources
	Machine Retrieval of Information
Application of Basic Functions by Clientle	Problems and Trends in Academic Libraries
	2 courses from these areas:
Tool Skills	Research Methods
	Statistics
	Systems Analysis
	Computer Programming
	Additional courses in one of these areas:
Additional Specialization	Subject Fields
	Management
	Foreign Languages

THE PREPARATION OF TOMORROW'S PUBLIC LIBRARIAN: SOME PROPOSITIONS, PRINCIPLES, AND PROPOSALS

Dorothy Sinclair

Associate Professor
School of Library Science
Case Western Reserve University
Cleveland, Ohio

Four Propositions About Change and the Future of Library Education

Proposition I: *It is specifics that change rapidly. Basics are more stable. We ask the same questions about new situations.*

When we consider the needs of education for public librarians of the future, we are not considering only what the public libraries of the future may be like, although that is, of course, a part of the problem. Other questions that arise concern such topics as: What education is needed by the beginner? How much should be taught by the school, how much on the job, how much at a later date in a sixth-year program? What skills and knowledge will, in the future, be contracted for outside the profession rather than provided by librarians themselves?

These and other questions which arise have a familiar ring. Even though they are being asked about librarians of the future, they are questions we have asked before: To what extent can and should we prepare specialists, given the tendency of librarians to move from one position to another? Should we try to satisfy employers or to satisfy our own ideas of what librarians need to know? This may resolve itself into the hoary theory-versus-practice dichotomy. And, accepting the importance of some contact with the realities of library life, shall we return to some form of practice work?

With the growing complexity of our lives and institutions, we can scarcely avoid preparing for some degree of specialization, and, however it is managed, some contact with real public libraries is important. None of these points is new. But, as some of the needs to be met will be new, and as the methods of meeting them may well be different, the preparation for meeting them will be different

68

also. Library education needs to continue to search for ways of accomplishing the following: preparing specialists with a strong generalist grounding; and engendering innovative approaches to old problems without at the same time producing librarians so out of touch with reality that they can be of no use to actual libraries.

Proposition II: *The future does not only happen to us. We can help it to happen.*

In considering these questions, with an eye to the future and a firm intention to keep tradition from creeping into the picture for its own sake, we must also bear in mind that the future of the public library is not something that is fixed and definite for the years to come—that, in fact, what we teach will have its effect on the future, make itself felt along with the other forces at work in society. To a degree, then, it is fair to consider what we think the public library of the future ought to be, as well as what it seems inevitably to be becoming.

Proposition III: *We cannot surely predict anything but unpredictability.*

The trends of today are not infallible guides. If we are hoping to influence the professional careers of young people beginning work in the next five years, let us say, we are looking forward at least 10 or 15 years. Granted that some of library education's force fades early, and that proportionally experience and the effect of supervisors and colleagues take over as a career moves forward, still we in library education have no business to be here unless what we teach has some kind of long-range impact. Looking 10 years ahead, then, we encounter the problem of the impossibility of predicting the nature and extent of rapid changes in our society. Ten years ago it was 1962; if we stop to examine what has happened since then, we realize how fast change has occurred, and how unpredictably. Our very value systems have undergone a good deal of soul-searching. Is there any reason to suppose that such change will not continue? We do not even know the answer to that question.

Proposition IV: *The certainty of change is the certainty we must build on.*

In this very uncertainty about the future and this strong probability of change, we have to base our education for future public librarians.[1] It is true that we know a few apparently definite facts—that there are fewer children coming along, but a bumper crop of adults in their 20s; that more people between 20 and 30 have college educations than is true of previous generations; that automation has revolutionized vocational training needs and eliminated many unskilled jobs. These are facts about the present with possible implications for the future. But these trends do not in themselves help us much. Even more than is true of other types of libraries, the public library's future is tied in with society's future, because society itself is the public library's potential public.

It is fascinating to dream about the future. Perhaps we will have a nationwide 800 telephone number which can be dialed by anyone, anywhere, for any kind of information. A great switching center would refer the call to the best source of information anywhere in the country. Or perhaps every airport will have a public library branch, so that those long waiting hours can be utilized for pleasure or profit—with the difference that you could take the book on the plane with you and return it to any airport or library in the country—or even abroad. To come a little closer to today, perhaps public libraries will be mandated and not optional—if so, we will need standards with real teeth in them and the librarians of the future will have to devise them. And surely in the not-too-distant future we shall be able to take public library service across the rivers and unseen lines which constitute our state boundaries, in order to serve most effectively the natural communities which so often straddle state lines. The librarians of the immediate future will have to untangle the legal complications. And even today we should have state-supported or federal-supported migratory library service to follow the migrant workers in our midst as they move with the crops and the jobs.

Those developments are possible, but they may be wide of the mark. We should be wrong to prepare future public librarians in those specific directions, or in any specific directions someone else may envision for the future. What we must try to do, rather, is to prepare for a future with these and other potentialities, a future different in ways we cannot now predict. If this is true, we must help our students to discern the difference between ends and means, for it is only the latter that are unpredictable, and we must teach our students to learn to handle change, in themselves and their libraries. To a great extent, the management of change implies social and behavioral skills. The social and behavioral component, therefore, will occupy a higher place in the priority list of education for public librarianship.

Social and Behavioral Knowledge:
Key to Communication and Flexibility

In searching for words to serve as a theme for this section, I have sought collective words—unity (not uniformity), synthesis, integration, partnership. It is my belief that public librarians need to face the changing future with more communication and understanding within their libraries; more genuine unity with their communities; more two-way understanding with the official sector; and more and better communication among libraries and types of libraries. In the library education world, also, unity in diversity should be sought—in course content and teaching method. Liaison with other parts of the university would result in a more interdisciplinary program. Better methods of involving libraries and practicing librarians would be a part of the unified approach. And, finally, fuller cooperation among library schools themselves would make a highly desirable addition to a fully unified program on a nationwide basis.

This emphasis on unity, as what follows will show, does not minimize the needs for specialization, on the one hand, and the existence of genuine regional differences, on the other. Basically, what is proposed here is the infusion of a strong element of cross-fertilization into our various course offerings, plus a substantial element of behavioral material. Thus, the need for unity is tackled simultaneously in two ways: through unified course content, and through inclusion of sound behavioral knowledge leading to understanding and communication. In the public library world, as in the larger one, if we can solve the human problems, we can together tackle almost any other problem, including whatever the unfathomable future may have to offer.

At the risk of extreme redundancy, let us begin with two facts: the public library is *public*, and the public library is a *library*. The public nature of the public library implies two things: 1) that it serves, or is available to serve, the whole public, the entire community; 2) that it is a public agency in the sense that it is paid for out of tax money, that it is accountable to the taxpayers as all publicly supported services are, that it is in what we usually refer to as the public sector.

The public library is also a *library*. Today, that word is not as easy to define as it used to be. It is no longer solely book-oriented; it has long since ceased to be a storehouse; and nowadays it is increasingly detaching itself from a building. What "it" is—just as what its surrounding community is—has been, and will continue to be, subject to change. However, we know that its function is related to the collection, organization, and distribution of information, although "information" is too narrow a word to describe all the reading and viewing and listening materials which form part of the public library's stock in trade.

The particular point I want to make, however, with regard to the public library as a library is its relationships with other libraries. Cooperation among public libraries, usually in formally-organized systems, is a commonplace today. Increasingly, too, we hear of cooperation among types of libraries, including the public library. This second type of cooperative organization is more discussed than implemented; even where it is operational, it has not developed to the degree hoped for.

The Library and Its Public

Age Level Divisions

Current library education, like much current library organization, divides its service first among age-level lines. Children's service is usually clearly distinguished. Young adult service appears somewhat less so, but it can still be discerned in many libraries and library schools. Adult service, paradoxically, is often given without any special identification or planning. Adult services courses in library schools may tend to stress current special areas, such as the poor or the aging, rather than the total adult public, or may focus on group services in general.

This division has its obvious advantages, but it has also some equally evident drawbacks. Everyone begins as a child, but no one can specify the exact date on which he ceases to be one. Equally, we are seldom able to declare that, while on Tuesday we were young adults, on Wednesday we have become adults. Yet, in both library schools and the libraries for which they prepare staff members, there are often major variations in philosophy, policy, and approach in the three common age-service sectors. The actual human being, who at various points in his life has to use two or three of these services more or less simultaneously finds himself puzzled, confused, sometimes embarrased and angry.

Add to this the fact that the library school student frequently has to serve a different age group from the one he is trained for, and we have a need that seems

71

to look toward an integrated type of service, considering the whole man at least in spirit—a service consistent within itself, of which the parts form a meaningful whole. Library education, therefore, should make an effort toward preparing students for an integrated type of service in public libraries as regards age. This does not mean, as I hope to show later, that the special characteristics of each age will no longer be recognized and taken into account, but it does mean that some of the artificial barriers, which create confusion for the user as he grows from a child to a senior citizen, should come down.

There is an analogy here with medical education and practice which, while they move toward specialty in the later and more advanced courses, begin with the whole man. At the medical school of my own university, each beginning medical student is early assigned to assist in the prenatal care of a pregnant patient, and continues to follow the medical needs of mother, child, and family in general through his entire training. Whatever his later specialty, this early association with the normal needs of an everyday family prevents an undesirable narrowness of view.

Subject Specialist versus Generalist

Larger public libraries are now divided, especially in their main buildings, by subject—usually for adults and young adults. These subject divisions follow the classification as a rule, and run into the same difficulties as do makers of classifications as times and topics change. The subject orientation of our libraries is also influenced by the academic atmosphere from which most libraries arose. Even the public libraries of an earlier day were academic in a general sense—that is, they served an educated class who continued reading books of an educated sort. The public library itself has long since moved into broader spheres, but the subject classifications, which create the divisions, remain.

Here, again, there are many practical reasons why this arrangement is workable, and why library schools continue to offer courses on the literature of science and technology, etc. (In the latter case, one obvious reason is the need of students bound for university libraries.) But, in the nature of the case, the subject specialist librarian and the subject-oriented course may overlook the needs of the less sophisticated member of society. The common response to these problems has been that the less sophisticated reader will use the branch libraries or the "popular" or "home reading" part of the main library. This solution creates a problem in its turn, since the generalist librarians of these agencies have the defects of their virtues, just as do the specialists. For example, while the generalists may be more easily approachable for the unsophisticated, and more concerned with readability than conversant with the latest and most accurate information, surely no library wishes to have to compromise in this direction. Such a compromise involves, in the long run, a patronizing decision that for these particular readers accuracy and currency do not matter. Here, then, is another area in which integrative influences through library education are needed.

Innovative versus Traditional

Even more special than the needs I have so far mentioned are those of the so-called disadvantaged. Here, we are in an area singularly ill-defined, including different minorities in different parts of the country, with variations in language ranging from "Black English" through Spanish, to a variety of American Indian languages spoken in some regions. But ethnicity is not in itself the only criterion for such special services. In many communities, the distinguishing characteristic is undereducation, with functional illiteracy at best. Along with these, and frequently found simultaneously, is economic poverty. In all communities identified as being in need of special library programs, there is a life style and a set of values different from those of middle-class Americans.

In many places library education and library practice have tackled these problems whole-heartedly, often aided by federal funds. A current federal emphasis is on ethnic cultural centers, with a large measure of genuine community control. Studies have apparently shown that programs of this type are more successful when divorced almost entirely from the other services of the parent library, because of obvious variations in clientele, approach, rules, etc., etc.[2] Here is a cleavage in the public library world whose barriers are stoutly defended—as, indeed, would be the others already noted.

But I should like to ask two questions: First, how long-range are the programs now supported by federal funds? We do not know how they will fare when the outside income ceases, but presumably economies will have to be made and administrative adjustments arrived at. Furthermore, are the long-range goals of these programs completely divorced from the "traditional" service? Surely some, at least, of the needs of users of the new programs will best be met by use of the total library resources and specialists, especially when, as we all hope will be the case, illiteracy and undereducation gradually yield to the current efforts to eliminate them. In short, the best long-range service to the special communities noted may not be precisely what is now available in crash-type programs.

Secondly, it is apparent that the new programs are discovering a good many useful techniques and opportunities for service which are appropriate for a wider clientele. Some method of communicating these discoveries and adapting them to other neighborhoods is needed.

And finally, *why* is it true that "traditional" libraries and innovative programs for the poor seem to have difficulty in mixing? Some of the reasons are deeply imbedded in our social systems. But some are library-related reasons, and thus amendable to change through a differently structured and differently oriented library education. Here, too, then, it appears that we need unifying influences in library education and in libraries themselves.

The Public Library and Government

The situation here varies tremendously from state to state and community to community. Some of the situations I shall mention will not apply everywhere. Certain trends of government can be discerned, however, and certain characteristics of libraries, or at least some libraries, can be identified.

The tendency of government most painfully apparent to library administrators today is probably PPBS or some other aspect of program budgeting, involving the concept of accountability and measurement of results. This movement is relatively new to local government, and will probably continue for some time. It creates obvious barriers to communication when budget

73

justification is in question because of the difficulties of measuring library outputs. Whether they like it or not, however, public libraries are going to have to try to communicate with governments in these terms.

Complicating the picture is the situation of most public libraries which operate at one remove from local government. In extreme cases, this cleavage takes the form of a library board and staff who pride themselves on "keeping out of politics" and feeling quite aloof from the rest of the publicly supported agencies.[3] Often this posture is combined with an elitist and literary group of Friends of the Library who, while they are pleasant people who give genuine financial help, tend to place the library in official eyes in the same category as the solely "cultural" agencies such as the symphony of the art museum. The fact that local government is one step removed from the library because of the board, combined with the impression that non-user officials may have of the library as literary, elitist, and semi-philanthropic in nature and support, creates an unhealthy climate in which the administrator must meet the budget analyst and city councilmen with requests for funds. Here, too, then, we need bridges to overcome barriers. Library education has a responsibility to assist students to understand, communicate with, and influence government officials.

With other government agencies, too, many libraries need to establish better liaison. As libraries begin to give information and referral service of a different kind, as they attempt to make their services more meaningful to the recipients of welfare and remedial education and job retraining, they need better communication with those who perform these several services. Much has been done in many communities, but elsewhere the library's semi-isolation has effectively cut it off from easy access to these professionals who should be colleagues. It is true that this type of liaison has its dangers, for in some communities the public is hostile to government agencies, and the library must beware of cutting itself off from groups of citizens by too-close identification with "the establishment." The library staff must learn how to identify with all segments of its community. Certainly library education has, in many schools, given attention to this need, but more and better guidance in this type of liaison is needed for the future.

The Public Library and Other Libraries

In both library operation and library education, the systems movement has been emphasized. Interlibrary cooperation has ceased to be merely a topic of conversation and has become a reality. Like any other theoretical concept which is translated into factual terms, it has developed a new set of problems. As library systems grow in complexity, their structures become complex, also. New types of boards, or advisory committees, or administrators' councils are set up. Here, we meet such problems as large versus small libraries in the same system, with thorny questions about representation within the system, sharing of costs, and prickly feelings to be considered; or problems of "host" libraries housing "guest" system staffs, with the host tempted to consider the staff its own and the other system members convinced that the host library gets more than its share of benefits, while the host may go uncompensated for generously offered space. These behavioral and organizational problems need skilled attention by experts, and library education should tackle them, along with the automation and collection-building aspects of the system problem.

When cooperation moves beyond public libraries, and embraces school and academic libraries in some formal structure, communication and understanding create even tougher problems. Each has its own philosophy and value system appropriate to its own clientele and institutional structure. Inevitably there are differences, and cooperative service falters when their variations are not understood. Surely the place for such communication to begin is the library school, which prepares its students for the various types of service, and which should be able to clarify and delineate these differences as a first step toward understanding and meaningful cooperation.

Some Suggested Courses

A Course on Human Development and Human Information Need

This course might be taken by everyone in the public library program. Each student, however, would opt for a different emphasis: young children, older children, teen-age, the poor, nonspecialist adult, specialist adult (business, labor, helping professions, government), older adult. The class would meet as a whole perhaps for every third session, with the specialist groups meeting separately for the remainder of the time.

The general sessions would consider man from babyhood to old age—his social characteristics, his ability to learn, his roles in society, the information need generated by each role. Reports from the sections would supplement lectures. Faculty from non-library disciplines would be called upon to give some lectures—educators, sociologists, psychologists, etc. Application of the general session content to specifics would be discussed in the sections.

Ideally, the general course should last all year, the children's sections should meet during the first term, and the adult sections during the second. Realistically, however, the exigencies of schedule-making may eliminate this possibility. Within the sections there would be a more concentrated attention on the specialization chosen, with emphasis always on the human being, his roles, and his information needs. For example, in the case of adults, roles would include family member, householder, local citizen, national and world citizen, physical being, spiritual being, member of groups and organizations, consumer, etc. Materials learned in other courses with emphasis on subject (reference, materials selection) would be brought to bear here on the human needs which the librarian will meet in practice.

The course as outlined would hope to preserve the necessary special attention to the characteristics and needs of age groups and other community groups, but at the same time would call attention to the fact that the age groups represent a continuum rather than a series of disparate segments, and that there are, in all the groups, many common characteristics. Such a general background will be of value to the student whose future work brings him into contact with many segments of the community, of all ages. There is a great need today, and in all probability tomorrow, to try to ease the age barrier. Today's young people, admirably tolerant of other races, cultures, religions, and life styles, are often quite intolerant of older people from their own culture. If the young librarians now being educated are to serve the "over 30" population effectively, they will need to develop better modes of communication, based on better understanding, with this group also.

A Course in Communication: Theory, History, Practice

This offering, which would be more broadly based than the purely public-library-type courses, could, in fact, be required of all students. It would take the place in the curriculum of the history of books and libraries course, some part of which would be included. It would add, however, some of the theoretical aspects of communication—not only a brief introduction to communication theory of the epidemiological, mathematical type, but also in more detail the theoretical approach to human communication between individuals and in groups. The practical aspect would take the form of sensitivity training, including listening and interviewing. Actual practice could take the form of communication among students planning specialization in public, academic, and school librarianship about cooperative services, and among public library students planning to specialize in widely differing services, such as subject department work, children's service, poverty programs.[4] Tapes would be used, and student communications diagrammed and discussed in class. The experience would provide practice in communication *per se*, while the content would be related to library communications problems.

Management Course

There is a tendency in modern library education to consider management without regard to type of library.[5] Certainly some aspects are common to all libraries and to other types of organizations as well. But the public sector is different in so many ways from private management, and managing a separate agency is so different from managing a library which is part of a larger agency (a university, a school, a company) that some attention to public library management *per se* is needed.

Here again, perhaps it would be possible to give a course which combined in general sessions the concepts applicable to all, and then to divide a large class into sections for specialized attention to the management problems of the public, academic, school or special library. General principles of the systems approach, of supervision, of good personnel procedures, etc. could be covered in the joint sessions. In their special section, the public librarians would consider civil service, preparation and justification of public library budgets, public library law and legislation, working with boards and citizens' advisory committees, the pro's and con's of community control; centralization versus decentralization of service; experiments in extension work as alternatives to branches—such as the caseload method used in Project Aurora, or the mail order catalog. Actual practice in budget preparation and simulated budget hearings could be included. Here law school practice of moot court proceedings is a precedent.

While there is some feeling in library education circles that management should not be taught to master's level students, enough of them move very soon into responsible roles (heads of small libraries, middle management or second in command in units of large libraries) that this type of training is definitely needed. There seems no reason to suppose it will not be needed in the future, especially in view of the trend toward participatory management which will involve many staff-members in non-managerial posts in the decision-making process.

Many of today's young people—and library students are now coming largely from the young, just-graduated group—are totally uninterested in budgets and management *per se*. To some, this is all part of the system which they wish to ignore or supplant. Many have an unrealistic idea about the resources available to government, and believe that there is some sort of conspiracy to keep public funds from being put to really good use, for the benefit of the people. It is to be expected that these young people will indeed make changes, but library education will be remiss if it does not attempt to acquaint them with the facts of public sector life, and arm them with the ammunition they will need to secure better support for libraries, as well as introducing them to sound methods of planning for change and bringing it about through whatever legal or administrative measures are necessary.

Specifically, library education needs to infuse into its curriculum, if it has not already done so, a hard-headed approach to objectives, to measurement of results, to presentation of alternative roads to the same result, and especially to ways of stating all these points in terms of the overall objectives of government. Many libraries can tell how many books in the 600's circulated, but how many can tell how many materials were used, both in the library and at home, on the subjects of drug abuse or pollution control? Which of these figures would be more meaningful to an official? This example is given not as a specific that should be taught but as an example of a type of thinking—how to express the library's program in terms which are meaningful to officials and consistent with officials' larger goals.

Other Course Content Related to Liaison with Government

In addition to the management course, with its special emphasis on the library's posture *vis-à-vis* government in official relationships, the program suggested makes other contributions toward service to, and cooperation with, service-oriented public agencies. In the human development course, it was suggested that information needs of, and service to, government might be one of the optional section offerings. Another was concerned with the helping professions—usually, though not always, public agency personnel. A recent study has shown that this group does not make great use of libraries;[6] apparently libraries need to be better informed about their activities and information requirements in order to be able to offer meaningful service. In both these sections it was assumed that outside speakers from the university and the community would add to student understanding and ability to communicate. Public libraries can, and some do, give a service to local government which almost approximates the state agencies' service to state government, or even the Library of Congress's Legislative Reference Service.

Such service, in addition to its contribution to the community through an informed officialdom, gives officials a better insight into the nature of a library and its services, on the one hand, and gives librarians a better understanding of the concerns and general posture of government, on the other.

Inter-Session as an Aid to Flexibility

For certain special needs requested by the profession but difficult to fit into the crowded curriculum, the currently popular 4-1-4 scheme offers a convenient solution. Inter-session of a month in January may be utilized for mini-courses on such how-to topics as book talks, operating AV equipment, puppet shows, and so forth. It can also be used for practice work on the part of students without library experience, and for field trips to libraries in other parts of the country. Another valuable use is the student-initiated organization of "think-tanks," in which students stretch hard for solutions to current library problems, sometimes thereby arriving at projects which can be carried forward into the spring term as independent study projects for credit.

Effect on Traditional Master's Courses

One of the advantages of the special courses outlined would be that they would permit the traditional courses to be taken by public library oriented students along with the remainder of the student body. Reference, for example, could be given to all, since the public library group would have the opportunity, in the human development course, to relate the content of the course to the specific groups studied. The same is true of materials selection.

Cataloging and classification are skills with which every librarian needs some familiarity. Not every public librarian, however, needs to be prepared to be a cataloger. Some will need the full course; others (preparing for children's service, outreach programs, etc.) may perhaps be given a short intensive course during inter-session.

Other commonly-offered courses are subsumed in the suggested curriculum offerings—management, library in the community, history of books and libraries, public library systems. Some are curtailed, it is true, and should be available in fuller form as electives for students with a special interest and need, perhaps as "independent study" topics.

Library Education for Non-Librarian Specialists

There are certain kinds of borderline specializations which, beyond the general coverage in general courses, need to be considered. As an example, let us consider the preparation of the supervisor of service to the poor. For this position, which involves supervision, planning, and administrative community contacts in connection with referral services, a senior staff-member with a social work background is felt by many libraries to be ideal. The holder of this middle management position needs library skills in order to bring them to bear on the service and also in order to take his or her place within the library organization as head of a service. Do we give additional training in social work to a librarian? Or do we give a short course on the background concepts of the library to a social worker? Either of these options is possible; probably either would work with the right person.

If, however, we decide on the short course in librarianship for the specialist in social service, the same course might well be useful to other specialists within the library who come well prepared in their own fields but who need exposure to the library way of life and thought in order to perform successfully as library personnel officers, library public relations officers, non-librarian administrative aides to library directors, systems analysts and other high-level specialists employed by the larger libraries and multi-library systems. Such a course might also be taken by members of management consultant firms and others concerned professionally with libraries but not as librarians *per se.*

Effect on the University as a Whole

Many of these suggestions imply interdisciplinary cooperation within the university, especially with faculties of social and behavioral sciences and management. There would be complications about this in many universities, but perhaps some departments could be persuaded to accept a *quid pro quo* in the form of instruction in library use and materials in the department's discipline, given to its own graduate students (or others) by a member of the library school faculty.

The "Practice Work" Problem

The place of practical library experience as part of professional education has undergone several phases. Recently, after a period of being out of favor, it has begun to be accepted again as desirable. These vicissitudes may well reflect, first, the former need of library education to divorce itself from the image of vocational training, and second, the employment situation during the manpower shortage, when library positions were filled by people without degrees, who later entered master's programs with experience behind them.

Reasons for the infusion of an element of the practical are self-evident to the supervisor of the new graduates, who complains that certain skills and knowledge have been overlooked. The increasing complexity of theoretical knowledge, the greater diversity of specializations, the impossibility of preparing a student for one specific position in one specific library, are some of the reaons for this dissatisfaction which can never be resolved. If a person is to be prepared to hold a specific position in an individual library, a good case might be made for the superiority of on-the-job training. What professional library education attempts to supply is breadth of scope (what is the basic function? how may it be handled in different ways? what are the pro's and con's of each?). In so doing, the library school is preparing the student to meet change, to make a greater long-range contribution to the library of his choice, at the expense of preparing him for the specifics he will meet in the immediate situation. Practice work may help prepare him for day-to-day realities, as well as add the dimension of a laboratory-type experience to complement his theoretical education.

From the viewpoint of one who has been on both sides of the practice work picture, the two- or three-week experience has grave weaknesses. From the viewpoint of the cooperating library, the time is too short to prepare the student for meaningful work. Since the library's chief responsibility is to its public, it cannot jeopardize public service in order to give students an experience, nor can it afford the total supervision necessary for a one-to-one on-the-job tutorial type of relationship. Ideally, therefore, the practical component of library education should be of some duration. Ideally, too, it should take place in a good library under a good supervisor. The library school should have some control over these circumstances, and attempt to merge teaching, study, and the practical into a meaningful whole.

The comments to follow focus on several different types of practical experience which may be made available to students, some of which fall short of the ideals noted above.

Work-Study Experience

The economic situation may bring, in the immediate future at least, more part-time students to library schools. Many schools have deplored the necessity for part-time attendance, and there can be no doubt that the demands of a part-time work schedule and study schedule taken together add up to more than a full-time load. Periods of heavy work and fatigue are likely to coincide in the two spheres, and transportation and hours of either activity complicate the picture.

That is not to say, however, that the profession might not make a vitrue of necessity and capitalize on the need of students to work part time. Is it possible to eat one's cake and have it, too? Can a student both gain the benefits of part-time work (financial and educational) and at the same time sacrifice few, if any, of the values of full-time attendance at library school? There are one or two possibilities, not necessarily new, which might at least help toward these goals.

1. If the program involves the large library, a possibility to be considered is the technique now used by some industries in cooperation with universities—that of closed-circuit TV courses beamed to the library and taken by small classes of library staff. Costs might be a problem, and in some states the libraries might run into legal difficulties, but if they have the equipment for other purposes, this plan would eliminate the expensive travel time for the student staff member, and perhaps enable him to plan his study program more effectively, with less attention to timing of course offerings.

2. Cox-and-Box positions. This idea, not new, permits two people to hold one job and attend school, finishing in twice the normal time. The classified position is a regular one, with fixed salary, etc., and each incumbent holds it for alternate terms, attending library school while his *alter ego* works, and vice versa. If details can be worked out, these teams can even occupy the same apartments alternatively, at work and at school locations, respectively. This arrangement has the advantage of being applicable to people who do not live and work in a city which has a library school.

Internships

Some years ago Dr. Ed Wight recommended at an Institute of the Graduate School of the University of Chicago[7] that an internship in an approved full-service library be required of every student. There can be no doubt that this would be valuable, but the suggestion was not widely adopted. Perhaps, in view of the changing manpower situation, it should be considered again. The University of Texas has offered an internship of a year as an optional alternative to a master's essay in recent years. Under this program, the student worked an academic year, received a salary the same as or slightly less than that of a new professional, and participated fully in the work of the library. The library agreed to assure opportunity to become acquainted with various aspects of the service, but since the student was to be on the staff for a long period, the library's cost in staff time for training and its problems of scheduling were justified. The student's report to his library school was a requirement for the degree.

Such a program has not been feasible elsewhere in recent years, because there were so many openings that students were badly needed for regular positions; but perhaps the climate of today would be right for an internship-type arrangement. The academic year of practical work would be required for the degree, and would therefore be to some extent supervised by the school. The school could, at least, approve in advance of the contracting library and require a report from the student. From the student's viewpoint, the opportunity for a year's assured employment, at or near beginning salary, would be welcome in these days of employment difficulty. The experience would presumably help in the later search for a permanent position, would provide a work reference, might perhaps lead to a permanent position in the library in which the internship took place.

The main problem in such an internship would occur in the library. An opening must exist in most libraries before a new employee may be added. Given the choice between an intern and a graduate librarian seeking the same post, the library might well prefer the latter, especially as the agreement about type of experience would not be necessary, and as the library would hope to invest its training and orientation efforts in an employee who might remain longer than eight or nine months. Nevertheless, if the internship program has value, today is as good a time as any to mount it successfully. Perhaps state library agencies could assist—by identifying libraries meeting certain criteria for internships, putting library and school in touch, or even by adding internship programs themselves in some cases. State libraries often have need of professionally educated personnel for short-term demonstration projects or special new programs. Working under good supervision on such a project would be wonderful experience for good young librarians.

The Practicum as a Major Element in Two-Year Programs

Many of the difficulties of accommodating practical experience, as well as course content, disappear if the program of library education at the master's level changes to a two-year one. Currently at Case Western Reserve, an experimental two-year curriculum to prepare students for service to disadvantaged communities includes a large element of practice work, not only in libraries, but, equally importantly, in community agencies. At the time this is written, the program has barely begun, but plans envision the placement of each student in a library-plus-community agency situation. Each student will work part-time in both types of agency, and the two will be in the same neighborhoods. It is true that different types of agencies will be encountered by different students, but a decision to sacrifice diversity in favor of in-depth and meaningful experience was made on the recommendation of the site supervisors. Interchange among the students will provide some diversity.

In addition to its advantage in permitting meaningful practical experience, the two-year program also enables both school and student to enlarge the scope of experience to include the highly desirable community agency work. This need is greatest, perhaps, in programs for service to inner city and "disadvantaged" populations, but there may be a possibility here for all public library bound students. In a two-year program, practice work could be involved with many of the institutions, organizations, and other services with which the library cooperates, and which it serves. The trend in Canadian schools toward a two-year program may be followed by American library education. If so, the type of practicum described could well be accommodated.

The Other Side of the Coin

In the previous comments about practice work, it was recommended as an antidote to the theoretically-based library education program which, it was noted, must be broader in scope and context than the individual library's services. Such a comment does not, of course, constitute a criticism of any library, nor fail to take into account the realities of budgetary, building, and community problems that all libraries must face.

Almost inevitably, practical experience taken concurrently with classroom work takes place in or near the same community. Often this is the student's home town. It thus tends to reinforce the student's natural assumptions that this library's operations, policies, etc., constitute a norm. If the school's faculty is also drawn from the same background and is best acquainted with the same types of library situation, the total educational experience may be too narrow. It becomes especially necessary, in such a case, for the faculty consciously to broaden its own knowledge and experience.

Another possible method of avoiding the in-breeding which may occur through localized experience is planned interchange of faculties among library schools—not for a whole term, since this merely gives some students a different teacher, but during terms, so that the student could have the benefit of both viewpoints and both backgrounds.

In many situations, the cost of this type of change (I had in mind a week or two in residence) would be prohibitive. But there are many library schools close enough to be able to manage it. Unfortunately, this interchange with faculty of nearby schools would not have all the values sought. For broadening, it is desirable to bring in someone from another region, to enrich the program with first-hand experience with its libraries, laws, officials, and library way of life. The variations are indeed great from state to state, and students acquainted with only a local library through experience need exposure to others in as meaningful and vivid a manner as possible.

Summary and Conclusion

A combination of old and new, this paper suggests that new wine can safely be stored in old bottles only if the bottles (here both libraries and library schools are intended) undergo changes which make them appropriate vessels for their changing contents. The ability to manage change is suggested as the major need of tomorrow's public librarian, and a strong infusion of library-oriented behavioral material is recommended as the best means of supplying that need. The task of the library school of tomorrow is well summarized in the Proposed Public Library Goals Feasibility Study, by Allie Beth Martin:

> Among public librarians there is a critical need to know:
>
> 1. How to determine the library and information needs of each community.

2. How to develop plans—set goals—*with*, not *for*, users.

3. How to communicate what the library is doing so that it becomes truly visible.

4. How to manage libraries so effectively that they will receive needed support.

5. How to perform actively, not passively.

6. How to change and help others to change.[8]

FOOTNOTES

[1] Two appropriate quotations appeared in the background paper, "Developing General Understanding of Library Potential," by R.J. Blakely, distributed at the 1963 American Library Association Conference, and published in *Student Use of Libraries; An Inquiry into the Needs of Students, Libraries, and the Educational Process* (Chicago: American Library Association, 1964), pp. 97-98. Kenneth E. Boulding is quoted: "Now we must develop an almost new form of learning. We have to learn from rapidly changing systems. Ordinarily we learn from stable systems." "After Civilization, What?" in *Bulletin of the Atomic Scientists*, XVIII (October 1962), 2-6. Alfred North Whitehead is quoted: "The rate of progress is such that an individual human being, of ordinary length of life, will be called upon to face novel situations which find no parallel in his past. The fixed person for the fixed duties, who in older societies was such a godsend, in the future will be a public danger." In his *Science and the Modern World* (New York: Macmillan, 1925), p. 282.

[2] Henry Drennan, "Library Information Center Projects and the U.S. Office of Education," paper presented at the 17th Allerton Institute, Graduate School of Library Science, University of Illinois. As yet unpublished.

[3] Oliver Garceau, in *The Public Library in the Political Process*, (New York, Columbia University Press, 1949) pointed this fact out years ago, and is one of many to have done so.

[4] Lawrence A. Allen, "The Education of an Adult Services Librarian," *ALA Adult Services Division Newsletter* (Fall 1968), 5-10. This article stressed the importance of behavioral education.

[5] Paul Wasserman states that: "The teaching of administration in library education appears to be very little advanced beyond the elemental level of a decade ago; the administrative process is still misunderstood, unknown, or ignored. A continuing proliferation of courses on special types of library provides ample testimony to this unchanged situation." "Development of Administration in Library Science," in his *Reader in Library Administration* (Washington, NCR Microcard Editions, 1968), p. 29.

[6] Vivian Cazayoux, *Public Library Services and Their Use by Professional Staffs of Welfare Agencies* (Madison, University of Wisconsin Press, 1967).

[7] Ed Wight, "Implications for Personnel," in Chicago. University. Graduate Library School. *New Directions in Public Library Development*, (Chicago, Univ. of Chicago Press, 1957), p. 94.

[8] Allie Beth Martin, *A Strategy for Public Library Change: Proposed Public Library Goals Feasibility Study* (Chicago, ALA, 1972), p. 52.

LIBRARY EDUCATION FOR THE FUTURE: THE SPECIAL LIBRARY

Loyd Rathbun

Library Officer
Lincoln Laboratory
Massachusetts Institute of
Technology
Lexington, Massachusetts

Introductory Comments

The broad philosophic goals of special libraries are the same as those of all other libraries; the specific emphases, aims, and techniques are different. While libraries other than "special" are rightly responding to the changing cultural demands for broader, less restricted materials, types of media, advanced technologies, and sophisticated services, smaller special libraries look forward to giving fundamentally the same services that they now provide.

For the large public academic libraries, the new vital elements to be integrated into their operations are computers, systems, and networks. To the special libraries, personal specialized service remains most important. When feasible, the special library will use the new hardware to advantage, but education for special librarianship must still give priority to individual intellectual competence for personal service.

It is my conviction and contention that, in order to prepare special librarians, the library schools need only to update curricula by adding certain appropriate and relevant subjects, and to include basic instruction concerning the library tools of automation. In this paper, I will be speaking of special libraries in general, which are sometimes large, but which most often have a staff of only one, two, or three persons. A special library may be in any institution having need for ready reference to recorded information, whether the institution be public, private, educational, or business. Subject categories are diverse: business, industry, technology, finance, insurance, publishing, public service, social science, etc. By definition, the special library has a specialized collection, serving a specific clientele, in active support of the work of its sponsoring organization.

The pollution of literary debris from the automation and information explosions fouls Libraryland. The literature which I read gives a plethora of predictions. Some of them are pure sensationalism. Most of them describe the newer technologies and warn librarians to get with it or else. We are told that in 2000 A.D. you will have a computer console in your office or at home through which you will use the library. (It says nothing about a friendly old console with tennis shoes). Long before the year 2000 (within the next 28 years) systems and networks will radically change all library operations. Information will be instantly available by electronics, and you can look at printed materials on a CRT whose signal is transmitted from a microform in some distant information center which is definitely not a Carnegie Library. (CRT is, of course, a "with it" abbreviation meaning a cathode ray tube, like a TV picture tube.)

These and many other technologies are coming; many are already here, and they are most impressive. But will they make the library user self-sufficient? I think not. The special librarian will still be around in the year 2000. He will still be anticipating information needs of his company, acquiring information materials, helping the client define exactly his wants. There will be sophisticated machinery and computerized services to use, but although these will be great and powerful, basically they will be modern forms of the librarian's standard tools. We librarians will continue to be the specialists in using these tools.

Because of smog on the crystal ball, the views expressed in this paper are basically those of the author, augmented by those of many friends equally enthusiastic about the continuing future of special libraries. The purpose of this paper is to envision from the viewpoint of special librarians just what special libraries may become during the next 30 years, and on the basis of this presentiment to make course and curricula recommendations for Library Education for the Future. Although this appears to be a straightforward, simple task, the special librarian hesitates to proceed immediately into it. Special libraries are too broadly varied, and a special librarian's work differs in so many ways from that of other librarians. Consequently, it is deemed necessary that the state-of-the-art be described rather completely in order to establish the importance of the curricula suggestions.

In recent years, many comparisons have been made of special librarians, documentalists, and information scientists. No matter how you define them, the really good librarian is all of them. To be called an information scientist may be important if it results in a favorable salary differential, but the job advertisements asking for services of an information scientist usually state that an MLS is required. For the purpose of this paper, the term "special librarian" means also documentalist and information scientist with whatever unique attributes these may connote. "He" stands equally for Ms. or Mr.; in special libraries the equality is more nearly recognized than many other places. The words "special library" will mean a center where information is gathered, stored, and distributed. It covers equally those libraries which are technical, business, government and humanities.

Special Librarianship: State of the Art

The Librarian

Predicting library education for special librarians for the next three decades is probably less risky than predicting it for public or college and university librarians. In the first place, most special libraries are business related; businesses are relatively stable in their organizational structure and in their way of operating. No major changes have taken place recently, and no revolutions are anticipated. In business or industry new interests, new products, new markets, and new concerns are always on the way. Adapting to these is routine and is one of the joyous challenges in the life of a professional librarian. These elements come in normal conservative progression. Courses to prepare the student for oncoming developments are new but not unusual or radical.

Secondly, the student who is planning, or even considering, going into a special library is probably by nature more business-like and more conservative. He is realistic in judging which academic courses will help him, and he also understands the need for "required" courses. When he sees that provision is made to instruct him in profitable new subjects and techniques, he is not apt to demand or even to wish for radical innovations.

The student preparing for a job in a special library will probably vary in other personal characteristics. Special librarianship requires a different personality. The special librarian msut be dynamic, aggressive, and able to operate under pressure. This does not mean that a public librarian could not have these traits. But the traits more characteristic of the public librarian are empathy, understanding, and patience with all ages, classes and intellectual levels. The special librarian must be more commercial. He must be alert to subtle changes in his company, its new fields, new products. He must be aggressive in obtaining materials quickly, and he cannot be hesitant in presenting them to the persons who can use them. He lives in eager anticipation of the "pressure" when, in order to meet "proposal" deadlines, his company suddenly develops an urgent need for library materials not easily found nor immediately available. The resourceful special librarian will find the information in his own library or get it by long distance phone calls, or a personal trip.

Librarianship for special libraries is basic librarianship, but special emphasis is put on certain aspects. Although usually smaller than the all-purpose collection in a moderate-sized public library, the specialized collection may contain everything known to be significant in the subject field. It may contain every conceivable type of media. There may be multiple copies of needed materials. It is intended to be a working collection, actually to be considered "tools" for the functioning of its proprietary organization. As in all libraries, the avowed purpose is service, but service in the special library is an active aggressive function. While the library works through individual clients, its aim is to be an integral part of the working organization, which has production goals to be constantly met.

Much of the description of a special library just given could easily fit a departmental library in a large public or academic facility. In fact it often does, and their librarians are often classed as special librarians. The distinct characteristic of a special library is its "function," which, of course, is the responsibility of the librarian and which is initiated by him. In short, it is the special librarian that makes the library special.

At this point, let us review other things which special librarians do. As we list the various activities, it will be noted that many are similar or analogous to those things done by librarians in all kinds of libraries. But remember also that the special librarian may be the only professional on a staff of two or three persons. Even when there are as many as three graduate librarians in a special library, there can never be a distinct separation of tasks; each of them will be doing *all* of the jobs listed below and more.

The special librarian will manage the library and its services in the sponsor's best interest. (It is a "working" unit in the organization or company; when it ceases to contribute, to "produce," it is no longer necessary.) The librarian acquires knowledge of the company's business by a positive plan and direct effort. This includes attending every possible company meeting: briefings, business and technical sessions, seminars, and lectures. He scans all available company reports of every kind, and he arranges to receive copies of papers and articles presented by members of the company staff. He makes sure that his supervisors understand his need for this information so that he may freely question them and so that they will forward information to him.

The Special Librarian and the Materials

On the basis of his knowledge of the company's business, the special librarian will establish procedures policy and then carry it out. Book selection involves not only relevance to company projects but the number of library users on the same projects and the urgency factor. In a profit-making situation, it is as intolerable to queue up for necessary books as it would be to queue up for mechanical tools on the production line. Similar judgments are involved in journal selection, but equally important to the decision may be the immediate availability of photocopies of selected articles from some large research library. The special librarian must also continually face the ever-expanding journal runs in a strictly limited allotment of space. Should he forever pack them in tighter? Can he afford microfilm?

A large percentage of special libraries are in science and technology. Technical reports are an important part of the working literature. The question: microfiche or hard copy (cost ratio 1:3)? Does the library supply the micro reading equipment for individuals to take to their offices? If there are government security classified reports, how shall they be handled in this particular library situation? Do we loan or give reports? Do we catalog or just forget them? They grow, flower, and wilt like weeds. Weeding them is another decision-making chore.

The special librarian is called on to obtain many other kinds of library materials: government legislation, committee hearings, reports, patents, odd pamphlets, tables, charts, maps of all kinds for everywhere, films and tapes, etc. Much of this requires creative imagination to know where to start phoning to find out who to call. When it comes, who pays for it, and should it be cataloged or not?

One other problem area in special libraries acquisitions is translations. A little knowledge and experience here can save considerable money and frustration, but it is hard to come by.

Services of the Special Librarian

In the area of service the special librarian has one distinct advantage over other categories of librarians—he is working with clients whom he knows and who know him. The clients are serious, have confidence in his demonstrated ability, and will tell him their needs as best they can.

The special librarian's most impressive service is that of searching. It may result in either an informal or a formal bibliography. It may take hours or days, and it involves all of the librarian's tools, technique, and experience. It may be manual, the old-fashioned way, or it may call on the retrieval services of NASA, DDC, ISI, and other taped data bases.

Another valuable service is variously called alerting or current awareness. It may also be done manually, or the librarian can subscribe to tape services; either way, the client is alerted to all literature appearing in specified places on the subjects of his stated interests.

As a by-product of all of this, one of the more distinctive services of the special librarian is his constant watchfulness for any unexpected material which he knows will be of interest professionally or personally to his individual clients. This service fills two functions: it provides material information which may be valuable to the client, and it builds an appreciation for and loyalty to the library.

There are many other small services which a special librarian may provide a specialized clientele, for example: names of who is working on what in the organization; where to get specific information or services in the company; names of various association members in the company; local book dealers; available public libraries, etc. While this sort of accommodation may not be a "chartered" service requirement, the good special librarian provides it to make the library indispensable to the users.

In the special library the emphasis is on service with speed. As materials or information must often be acquired on request (the needs cannot all be anticipated) and as the need is often urgent for the progress of a project, the librarian uses the long distance telephone much more freely than he would in a general library. Other procedures for shortening acquisitions time include standing orders, deposit accounts, use of several dealers, and compromise and agreement with the company purchasing department in order to use open accounts and cash purchase arrangements.

The Library

Our crystal ball and a little intuitive calculating have indicated that there are 6,000 to 8,000 special libraries in the United States that are recognizable as libraries and that have librarians in charge. On the basis of other observations we guess that there may be another 2,000 to 4,000 potential special libraries presided over by something like librarians. As technologies continue to advance and competition grows stiffer we can look for more company libraries to be established. It is already happening. Obviously, recorded knowledge is important to many progressive organizations, important enough to have handy at all times. It is even important enough to pay for. And as the progressive organizations grow and expand, they will need more library services.

The expanding technologies call not only for more information; they call for information in other fields; they may call for completely new information. In our developing culture, the information itself is becoming more sophisticated. As idea units of information continue to grow exponentially, so grows the cataloging and storage demands of these recorded idea units. As the sophistication grows, so grow the complexities of defining and retrieving. Gone are the days of the desk-top collection of all necessary reference material. Now here, and to come, are the days of special library service.

Even before the promise of automation, special libraries varied considerably in form, dictated by the needs of the sponsor. There always have been, and probably will be for years to come, traditional libraries of books and journals. Financial organizations may have a preponderance of file cabinets of pamphlets, reports, and clippings. Certain industries will depend almost entirely on technical reports. Through many variations, at the opposite end from the traditional is the "library" of a desk and telephone, without books but with a knowledgeable librarian and with borrowers' privileges from several major university, public, and industrial or association libraries. So when we consider "Library Education for the Future: The Special Library," we must consider the education of the special librarians for special library *service*.

The Hardware on the Way

There is probably some truth in the wildest of predictions about the future. Many things will be different from those we now know. Already there are operating computer networks between university libraries to share materials and hold down redundancy. So far, justifying the cost is the biggest problem. The Bell Telephone Laboratories have their catalog and circulation system in the computer for three libraries at some distance from each other. Sharing materials is again the major purpose. Other network experiments are constantly being announced. Many libraries, both large and small, have effective operating systems for catalog, circulation, and serials control. A few have complete computer systems which, from one input, can place an order, receive the material, process it, and eventually discard it—a kind of cradle-to-the-grave bibliographic care.

There are many information analysis centers now working throughout the nation. To my knowledge, they are all in the field of the physical sciences. But I believe that all of them have their data stored for retrieval from the computer. *Chemical Abstracts* has been able to add new services through computer manipulation. And there are some strictly private organizations, such as the Institute for Scientific Information, publisher of *Science Citation Index*, who make make output or tapes available on subscription. Incidentally, ISI has recently broadened out into the field of the social sciences.

We have grown accustomed to the idea of microfilm, aperture card, and microfiche. Now the development of the automated library combines the storage capacity and flexibility of microfiche for textual materials with the catalog retrieval capabilities of the computer and with electronic transmission of both to places remote from their storage.

The most advanced work I know of towards library automation is that of Project INTREX at M.I.T. (INTREX is an acronym standing for INformation TRansfer EXperiments). It had been observed that virtually all of the computer operations in libraries are designed to do traditional library clerical chores better and faster than manually. Project INTREX was conceived to do something new—to develop library services not possible before the coming of the computer.

As stated in a project report, the experiments are concerned with the two main functions of any information transfer system: 1) bibliographic searching (the catalog) and 2) full text display. On a typewriter keyboard at the computer console you ask for a catalog entry much as you would consult the card catalog. A general subject request will bring you a long list of titles. A more specific limiting statement will reduce the size of the list. The lists will appear on a picture tube (a CRT). When you find a pertinent entry, at your option you can read all of the information which would be on an LC card plus much more. For example, there is the author's affiliation, the kind of article (e.g., professional journal article), purpose (e.g., theoretical and experimental), a complete table of contents, a bibliography if the article carries one, a detailed abstract of the text, and an unlimited number of extensively detailed subject entries.

If your search in the catalog reveals an article you wish to read, a simple signal will bring the first page of a microfiche to the picture screen. For obvious reasons, only short documents are available at this time, but the data bank has 20,000 of them, a respectable number quite adequate for real research. They are all within the field of materials science and engineering, chosen because of the importance and size of its literature base and because of the potential of actual student use which it would attract. (The computer is programmed to keep a history of the producers of each user for study by the project staff.)

This is the electronic hardware and its attendant services which we can see now and in the future in special libraries. They will be expanded and refined. Probably within a very few years we shall also hear of "great advances" in optical technology for storage and retrieval. It is promised as a step up in speed and storage capacity. It will still offer the same basic electronic accommodations but at optical frequencies.

The Library's Sponsor

Most special libraries are set up in organizations with active ongoing programs subject to growth, development, and expansion. Private companies, societies and associations, and government agencies can all be considered as conservatively forward moving with the times. Three elements appear most likely to have increasing influence on the content of library services: 1) The proliferation in subject fields and in technologies; 2) Interest and expansion into the international scene; and 3) Trend toward social awareness and activity (e.g., racial problems, urban blight, ecology).

It is easy to see these three elements separately affecting different ones of the types of organizations listed above. It is particularly interesting to note that one current trend in profit-making businesses brings them all into play—diversification. Competition at home and increasingly abroad, with various social pressures, has resulted in some remarkable combinations of industrial enterprises all under one head office. Imagine the potential information needs of the executive library in an organization such as a metropolitan fuel company whose corporate acquisitions since 1969 include (among other subsidiaries) large and varied real estate developers involved in property management and building construction, a home furnishings supply company, a mortgage company, a data processing service, an agricultural management organization, an automobile fuel conversion kit maker, and a leading mobile home manufacturer.

In the example, the diversification brought in a proliferation of subjects and technologies even if none was there before: international aspects appear with the large real estate activities and with agricultural and manufactured product export, and social concerns involving all of the examples in the third element above are evident in real estate management, agricultural production, the fuel conversion kit, and the mobile homes.

Special Library Curricula

Our most articulate leaders, the heads of most library schools, and many teachers and scholars have written often and much about the need to improve education for librarianship. Through both published papers and speeches they have spoken in advocacy of almost all of the things which I here present. But my recent study of the curricula listed in library school catalogs shows that very little has been changed in many years, and the unanimity in requirements and in course names and content is overwhelming. One can only hope that these present papers may stimulate action.

I believe that the curricula of library schools are by and large excellent. When the library student accepts it for the purpose for which it is designed, the course does function and does give him a background for professionalism. If, however, he demands relevance, he is asking for vocational training only. In the pithy words of Dr. S. I. Hayakawa, a "relevant" course nowadays means one which is intellectually empty.

We believe that a special librarian is first a librarian. A subject specialty may be an important part of his capabilities, but it is well recognized that during their careers most special librarians will work in several different positions, often in distinctly varied subject fields. So the basic courses, both philosophical and technical, which are common to all library schools' curricula, are essential to special librarianship now and in the future.

Format

The additions to the curricula which we will propose are suggested by the specific needs of special librarians, although some of them will be of interest to all librarians. For the education of the special librarian, however, we recommend using the curriculum format of the recent past. Through scheduled classes and formal presentations the vast store of factual matter, which is the librarian's personal data base, will be made directly available. A grading and credit system stimulates effort in the goal-oriented forward-looking student, and the resultant record assures a prospective employer of a certain level of intellectual achievement. The traditional format is flexible enough for a creative teacher to use freely; even if it is poorly used, there will still be value for the mature student.

General Education for Special Librarianship

As we consider courses or curriculum for the education of special librarians, we are again, as in the past, appalled by the multitude of viewpoints concerning what should be taught and learned. Students have for many years objected to certain courses as irrelevant to their future needs, although very seldom do students agree with each other about which courses they would omit. After they have worked as professionals for a few years they forget that there were "unnecessary" subjects, by which they have undoubtedly profited, and they are more apt to think of things which they had learned. As students, to many of them the word "professional" simply designates their occupational status after they graduate. For them, professional education and philosophy for librarianship has never been defined in any understandable form.

When we consider librarianship a profession, we are postulating that the primary basis is mental activity. John Boll has written:

> If librarianship were a trade rather than a profession, we would get away with learning and teaching only what is immediately useful. However, our claim to professionalism demands a wider range of thought, a framework or reference that is broader than the immediate work experience.[1]

Mr. Boll was speaking of librarianship in general, but his statement is equally significant for the special librarian.

The special library is established in those organizations which depend on recorded information. The library users themselves will be intellectually oriented, and they will look to the librarian as a scholar, knowledgeable in many things besides his specialty. To command their respect, he must have this "professional" background. Jesse H. Shera, at the annual Convention of Special Libraries Association in 1960, put it this way:

> Regardless of the library specialty, the librarian who is a scholar, irrespective of the branch of scholarship in which he may be trained, will succeed. All scholarship begins in mental discipline, and once the librarian has learned to master his thought processes, to observe phenomena accurately, to weigh evidence, to reject irrelevancies, and to evaluate conclusions, he will be a credit to his profession. Professional education, then, is the training of the intellect, upon which may be superimposed when necessary the 'tricks of the trade.'[2]

This statement concisely sums up the unspoken conviction of many of us. In 1972 there is no reason to modify in any respect the principles expressed by Mr. Shera. As a special librarian, I strongly urge keeping in the curricula those courses in library philosophy or history, and those principles of service which instill professionalism and a sense of loyalty to the profession. I add that the student *must* be told the purpose of such courses. So often we hear from recent graduates about courses "for which there was no reason or purpose whatsoever." As Mr. Shera says, "[The student] must be brought to an understanding of librarianship, the ends it serves, and the means it employs to achieve those ends, in the context of the society in which it operates."[3]

It is pleasant to consider oneself in a profession. Of course, there are those in our midst who question or challenge the statement that it is a profession. But it does appear that we have the potential: a vocation which includes the concepts of knowledge, skills, and attitudes. Many of our American leaders, through personal efforts, scholarly pursuits, and achievements, have qualified themselves for professional recognition. But due to lack of nationwide certification, the unrestricted use of the term "librarian" is possible. Although the MLS may be a hiring requirement in particular places, it still is jocularly spoken of by many as the "union card."

The special librarian deals for the most part with other persons who also have formal educations. When we compare our own background with that of members of some of the better recognized professions, we may feel inadequate. Our graduate-year-and-a-summer-session seems trivial beside long medical courses, exams, and internship, or the rigors of law study and the bar exams, or the concentrated theological study and the student pastorate.

A Pre-Library Course

Since the beginning of the first library schools, educators both in and out of library school faculties have often suggested the need for broader liberal arts education in addition to specific vocational training for the librarian. This need has not diminished over the years; it is constantly expanding, as are the fields of knowledge. Library schools depend upon the colleges of liberal arts to provide candidates for the graduate year. If a more inclusive liberal arts background is wanted, a closer working relationship between the colleges of liberal arts and the graduate library school may be in order.

A logical way to broaden the librarian's liberal arts education would be to establish a "pre-library" course of study and to include it in the university catalog. However, such a move would be of much more value than merely to "broaden the liberal arts education." An immediate benefit would be in making known to a new college enrollee the existence of a career in libraries. (To many persons, this is now completely unknown.) It would enhance the importance of the graduate year by suggesting that planned undergraduate preparation was necessary. And it could offer the opportunity for librarians, especially special librarians, to obtain a fundamental background in many more subject areas.

The basic intent of this pre-library course would be to broaden the librarian's fields of knowledge—not to affect the curriculum content of the graduate year except to make it more significant to the student. The first two college years would have the usual undergraduate liberal arts courses: basic English, history, mathematics, art appreciation, etc. The junior and senior years would include the "library major" and specific subject minors, or possibly a second major. The library major would consist of 18 hours of knowledge from several disciplines. Each would be a one-semester survey (or introductory) course on a separate subject. Some would cover the actual subject matter of the fields about which, in the graduate year, a course in "literature in the [subject]" might be given. Subjects could include arts, economics, history, literature, mathematics, biological sciences, physical sciences, social science, world affairs, and others.

The School of Library Science at Syracuse University, in combination with the College of Liberal Arts, does offer a specific undergraduate library course. Although an AB is granted, the work is positively directed toward the graduate year and the MSLS. The difference in what we suggest is the distinctive library major with a large variety of subjects. Paramount to it all is the acceptance and establishment of the pre-library course at all parent institutions of the library schools.

In spite of the fact that library schools have long required a liberal arts background with a few courses containing some of this same subject content, many of the undergraduates, not knowing the reasons for it, have completed and promptly forgotten such courses. This is a mild form of the drop-out syndrome: "I couldn't see any point in it." If emphasis were placed on the importance of a library major consisting of these many separate subject courses as preparation for the graduate year, maybe some students would get the point.

I must admit that I do not understand the many complexities of university departmental obligations, responsibilities, prerogatives, jealousies, and politics. But it would be very desirable to collaborate to establish an announced undergraduate pre-library course of study. Undoubtedly, a "major" consisting of several diverse unrelated subject courses, each at an introductory level, would be against all reason as viewed by the curriculum committee of a college of liberal arts. However, nothing could be more logical, effective, and productive for undergraduate preparation for library school. Furthermore, with astute planning, it is still possible for a student to program a strong specialized subject minor.

The pre-library course needs no more elaborating. Implementing it would require only agreement between the usual diplomatic library school administration and a cooperative dean of the school of liberal arts. The Syracuse University set-up offers a working example.

Automation Basics

Library automation is on the way in. It has not come as quickly as the enthusiasts predicted. Some of the promised miracle systems have not made it at all. But computers do clerical chores successfully, and there are very efficient and productive computerized indexes and alerting services available on subscription.

The sensible or cautious librarian has been continually accused by many computer buffs of being timid or frightened by the "threat" of the computer. Now they harangue that we must master the tools and languages of modern data processing if we are to communicate effectively with computer people who can. The opposite view is that we no more need to do that than we need to know how to repair our own typewriters. This opinion is reinforced by C. Walter Stone, speaking at an opening session of the ASIS Annual meeting in 1971:

> In short, I doubt the need for extensive mastery of computer languages, or even much understanding of technical skills upon which one relies when utilizing information, storage, and retrieval service technology. The case—to put it as simply as possible, is simply this—we shall not be employing nor supervising many such personnel directly. Computer terminals will be addressed in plain English or something equivalent and output will be similar, whether typed out in printed form or displayed on a cathode ray tube.

For a long time to come, probably the most extensive use of the computer for library work will be storage and retrieval of reference citations—work done manually in the past with published indexes and abstracts. Computer data bases already exist for many disciplines, and their services may be purchased for complete searches, or subscribed to for printouts of specific categories of information. These data services offer far greater coverage than any individual library or organization could hope to do, and special libraries will probably lean heavily on them for computer services for the next two decades.

Most of these data centers now offer direct accessibility to their tapes from a subscriber's own terminal. To use them, the special librarian must know how to address the computer. Just as in past years the reference librarian learned how to use the different source books most effectively, the new generation of librarians must acquire the skills to question many different tape data bases. In the past, the library student found the books in the school library. Now and in the future, he should be able to consult the media he will use on a future job; the school must make available to him real equipment in a laboratory environment. He should be able to experiment with a card punch and a computer terminal with keyboard and viewing tube. For laboratory use, these could be older models, available at lower costs; some equipment might even be available as hand-me-downs from some friendly industry. But it should definitely be operative, and the terminal should be connected to real data bases which would actually be used in practice assignments.

The special librarian must be able to justify and utilize data services. This calls for systems analysis studies directed at computer uses. Necessary to these are the first units in the course outline below.

What we do suggest then is a course in:

"Automation Basics"
    Feasibility study and systems analysis
    Flow charting
    Systems design
    Computer uses
        What it can do
            Cost analysis
        Statistics and other extra benefits
    Computer major components
    Enough vocabulary to talk intelligently about programming
    Laboratory work at the computer terminal

"Automation Basics," as proposed here, is a course which very possibly would appeal as an elective to many students in library school. For special librarians it is essential to understand the fundamentals of the several different units listed. This course would differ, at least in description, from the occasional courses in computer techniques and programming now offered; it would be less detailed, broader, more general, and introductory in order to give the student an evaluative understanding. For the librarian who later needs it, more detailed training in programming of exactly the right kind and language can be acquired in one of the separate courses given by IBM, ACM, AMA, etc.

A teacher for a course like this must be carefully chosen. Obviously, he must be well-versed in the subjects of the separate units. He will need enthusiasm for the present performance capabilities of equipment for automation, but he should be a realist prepared to tell it like it is: Computers are wonderful; their promise is great for the future; to any but the largest special library, however, in-house programming and operating costs will be far greater than the benefits would justify, so learn to depend on outside services.

Although the prognostication is that librarians will not need deep and extensive computer training to run libraries, it is observed that efficient and suitable programming and systems development for future use of computers in libraries does need the expertise of persons with a thorough knowledge of librarianship. This age has brought a new choice in kinds of work for a graduate librarian: first, the various kinds of libraries, and second, computer software designing, planning, and implementing in the production of automated library tools.

This kind of work is very challenging and satisfying to some persons. The suggestion here is that the library school thoroughly educate the student in all aspects of librarianship but that it leave the student's training for systems design to a computer expert after graduation.

Business Management for the Special Librarian

As companies have grown or expanded so have their special libraries. With growth of the libraries come more management functions to the special librarian. In the past, the one and only course in "Special Libraries" as offered by most library schools has been inadequate in its teaching of management problems and techniques. "Management" or "Administration" taught primarily for public libraries has been irrelevant. The following described course is much more needed right now; the expanding future will make it imperative.

> "Business Management for the Special Librarian"
>> Economics of profit making
>> Budgeting
>>> Preparing the Budget
>>>> Capital expenses
>>>> Operating expenses
>>> Living within the budget
>> Purchasing
>>> Techniques for speed
>>> Discounts
>>> Company Purchasing Dept. bottlenecks
>>>> What to do about it
>> Business records
>>> Bookkeeping, principles, format, procedures
>> Operational statistics
>>> Library use
>>> Cost analyses
>> Communicating with higher management
>>> Regular reports
>>> Keeping it informed
>> Library personnel
>>> Professional, paraprofessional, clerks
>>>> Interviewing
>>>> Training
>>>> Supervising

Personal relationships
Library/client
Intra-library
Public relations, business style

"Business Management for the Special Librarian" would be of interest primarily to prospective special librarians. As such, it could be given as an alternate to the administration courses offered by most schools. Although some of the elements in the course would in name resemble those in an administration course, the sizes of the libraries concerned are so disproportionate and the commercial factors so important here as to make applications quite different.

World Affairs and World Resources

A major and significant trend which is affecting special librarians is one toward more international contacts and involvement. Foreign contact alone is not new. Librarians have bought, borrowed, and exchanged materials for many years; our sponsoring companies have had overseas branches since the advent of big business. But suddenly we have found the world "shrinking." Because of advances in communications and in transportation, we are much closer together. Newly emerging nations, and some of the older ones, are asserting their economic and industrial independence. Our established international business enterprises are feeling various pressures and making changes. The closer contacts between an infinite number of cultures and value systems in the world are creating conflict and problems. The recent dialogues between the United States and China, and with Russia, presages more activity for us all.

One of the specialists, Nasser Sharify, anticipated this trend, when, in 1968, he wrote about the librarian, documentalist, or information scientist of the near future:

> He will have to know much, much more about world resources than we do; he will have to be much more of an expert on international bibliographies than we are now; he will need to have a thorough knowledge of major bibliographical indexing and abstracting activities of all governmental, inter-governmental, and private organizations, in all parts of the world. He should be able to understand much more than our graduates do today about the conditions of the foreign book trade, the practices of bookpublishers and booksellers, and the government regulations for book importation.[4]

Mr. Sharify suggested gradually putting into library school curricula very specific courses on international library sources and services. At some time these may be necessary, but the special librarian should have a more general background course on world affairs with appropriate library resources mentioned secondarily. This may be contrary to accepted library curricula which presents only "literature and sources" in non-library subject courses. But background for now and for the future must come from exposure to the current scene. A library school education for librarianship for the near future can do no less than offer whatever courses are necessary to educate the librarian specifically.

The nature of the subject does not lend itself to a course outline. A bulletin-type description would be thus:

> "World Affairs and World Resources"
>> This course is planned to prepare one for service in a special library where international activities, governmental, political, or economic, are significant to the operation of the library's sponsoring organization. The course will present an ongoing view of the current situation in the world, with any necessary review of contributing events of the recent past. Concurrent will be the study of the literature and sources of timely information. Analysis of international activities will provide aid in forecasting information needs.

The course in "World Affairs and World Resources" should be among the elective courses. While it would be among those of specific importance to special librarians, it should for obvious reasons be scheduled to be available to all library students. It could be most effective if presented by two persons—a stimulating expert on the current international scene and a librarian to tell of pertinent world bibliographic resources, literature, and reference material. Time should be divided equally between the two sections, and there should be no attempt to make either one an exhaustive presentation.

Library Practice

The only innovative curriculum element which is proposed here is neither unique or new. It is a substantial course of "Library Practice" that would benefit library school graduates immeasurably. It should be at least a three-semester-hour course for credit, to be paid for by tuition and to be supervised and graded or "evaluated" in the same manner as is good student practice-teaching for a teaching certificate.

On and off for almost a century speakers and writers have suggested some form of supervised training covering a significant amount of time. Such a program could only result in better librarianship, improved understanding, and more exemplary service. The librarian-to-be would meet head on and become comfortable with the technique and the tools of the trade. He would put into practice many of those things which he is learning in library school. The supervision would keep him reminded of the principles of service which are sometimes forgotten in the confusion of work in the new job.

After supervised practice, the graduate student would feel better prepared as a new employee. The employer would likely find the new librarian less naive and more capable. Multiplied by the yearly number of library school graduates, it is even possible that library clients might notice the difference.

According to Samuel Rothstein,[5] the idea of "practice work" goes back as far as the late 1800s, when it was almost a continuation of apprenticeships. It continued in library schools in various forms even into the 1940s in spite of a great deal of vocal opposition, which Mr. Rothstein thinks was based primarily on an attitude that the "practice" was "non-professional." In 1967 ten schools still listed some field work, but it was in varying amounts and mostly without

98

credit. Library practice obviously holds a very minor place in American library school curricula.

In contrast, Mr. Rothstein points out, the British feel that it is essential to have considerable "practical work." The University of Sheffield and the University of London both call for a year's library experience before admission, and the University of London requires a further 12 months of service in an approved library *after graduation* before its diploma is awarded.

That the value of practice work *per se* has not been completely discounted is proved by the movement in some universities to insert a few months of full-time "cooperative work-in-industry" into an engineering curriculum. How much better this is than merely to hope that the student will have worked before beginning a course! The interest and energy which are brought back to the remaining study are unique and unsurpassed.

John Boll has recently pointed out the great benefit which practice work gives to further formal education. He makes an excellent case, bringing in significant details and ideas, and his proposals should be read by anyone who is at all seriously interested. This particular paper begins on page 204 in the April 1972 issue of *Library Quarterly*.

Most American library schools make a gesture in the direction of exposure of their students to the real library. The minimum exposure I have heard of is a one-time walk-through in a college processing department. Other schools assign a few hours each at various stations where students are generously tolerated. At least one library school, that of the University of Missouri, expects some previous job contact. The catalog states, "Those students who have not had meaningful work experience in a library will be required to complete, in addition to the minimum program, a course in library practice." But there is no agreement at all among schools as to the general desirability of any scheduled work period.

Special librarians, particularly, must have a working knowledge of all of the techniques of librarianship. Surprisingly, the new graduate often goes right to work in a small company library where he or she may be the only librarian, often the only person. It was from one of those young persons that I heard about the walk-through technical session. She had unfortunately missed class on the walk-through day, and on her first day on the real job, an interlibrary loan form (something never before seen) surprised her. She did want to handle it in a way to foster the best possible communications; she had friends whom she could consult, so she quickly learned. But someone should have been responsible for introducing her to it and to other realities as part of her training. A library practice program would have been the natural way.

The larger, more significant, and lasting effect of serving an extended practice period in a selected operating library would be the favorable exposure to professionalism at its best, expressed in work attitude, client relationships, and productive service. Too often, this expression is lacking in a librarian simply because the librarian has never experienced it himself. For someone preparing to enter a special library the experience would be invaluable. Of course, his practice should be done in a special library. But select library practice should be equally valuable to every library student.

Library practice should be a three-semester-hour course required for the

MLS degree. Participating libraries should be carefully chosen to provide proper facilities and to guarantee real training-supervision in all basic techniques and in all service areas of library work. Compensation must be made to the library, with complete agreement that supervision and critical evaluation is an essential part of the contract.

A training and practice session would require longer continuous work periods than would be provided by the usual separate one-hour class times. The student and the supervising librarian must be free to set their own schedule. The time might be spread over the semester, or the 50 to 60 hours could conceivably be put in during a two-week period after all other classes had finished.

A student who formerly had varied and meaningful experience as an employee in a library could petition, with appropriate documentation, to have that work apply in fulfillment of the required course. If approved, he could then enroll in an elective course.

The matter of a library practice course is fraught with complexities. Logistical difficulties have probably been the reason for its general discontinuance in spite of advocacy by some of librarianship's foremost thinkers. One premise for its disappearance is that it became too difficult for the library school to find librarians qualified and willing to accept the students. Now, 15 or 20 years later, perhaps this has changed. More persons are writing about and discussing library education, library associations are speaking out about accreditation, teaching policy, and curricula, and individual librarians evince much interest in curricula and in the problems. Library directors or managers, and working librarians—keys to the success of a library practice program—may now be in the mood.

If library practice were again accepted as a desirable unit in the curricula, the implementation might be easier than expected. Universities across the land are establishing support groups of alumni and other interested persons who could provide real assistance in this activity. For instance, Libraria Sodalitas, support group of the School of Library Science of the University of Southern California, is a strong homogeneous group of congenial people mainly in the southern California area. Although the basic purpose of the organization is to give continuing aid to the school, the membership is primarily librarians, mostly U.S.C. alumni, and all of them enthusiastically eager to help. Nothing could be more logical than for a representative committee to handle the preliminary arrangements in securing suitable practice libraries, probably some of their own. If no school support group exists, the climate of the time suggests that a local chapter or contingent of one of the library associations would be as willing and able.

Current Problems in Society

Earlier we mentioned three current developments likely to stimulate needs for subject information in special libraries. We have covered the proliferation of subject matter, and the tide of internationalism in proposed courses. But the third cannot be as clearly defined. It was described as a trend towards social awareness and activity—e.g., racial problems, urban blight, and ecology.

These problems are examples only. At present they are most evident, but there are others which could become equally significant (drugs, gun control, etc.). Public concern becomes activated and our powerful communications media magnify, inflate and sometimes distort the issues. The special librarian will be involved and it is good for him to know a bit more than a mere reference source.

Library school is not the place for a "background" course in any of these. But perhaps an imaginative and well-read teacher might conduct a seminar in "Current Problems in Society," which could readily encompass almost any important major topic. Again, this would not be a bibliography course, but the subjects would have strong implications for librarians.

Odds and Ends

In this recent inquiry as to what other special librarians felt were needed for the future, I found several things about which library school students must be informed more completely than heretofore:

Library nets and network management. The words, in context of the technology of the times, are direct and assumed to be understandable. But "network" is no more specific than "library." Networks range from a simple telephone line, over which to discuss problems and ask solutions, to exotic computer time-sharing cataloging projects. It would seem that this could be studied in a course on "College and University Libraries" or perhaps in "Reference Sources and Services."

Computer subscription services should require no important mention in library education; the services are advertised. But most of the representatives are still enamoured of the awe which they can inspire when they quote thousands and tens of thousands of dollars as charges for their inestimable services. Those thousands echo so loudly that few persons hear that some of the companies also provide services at a relative pittance. New special librarians should be told, for example, that ISI can give a significant custom-programmed awareness or SDI service with reports delivered weekly for about $20 per month. This is one of several valuable services at a reasonable cost for a small library. These are library resources, and they should be made known to the student. Perhaps this should be incorporated into the course on "Technical Libraries," or it could be brought in to "Resources in Science and Technology."

Machinery for libraries. Another practical matter in which the student should be instructed is selection of machinery for the library. Most common are microform reader-printers, and photocopiers. Even at the largest equipment exhibit one can compare only a few different makes. Basics of judging and selecting, with reference to in-house servicing and maintenance, could probably be included in a course on "Reprography and Graphic Systems." But that course might attract only a small percentage of students. Would there be a place in "Administration"?

Where would the ethics of photocopying fit in? Is the "Administration" course large enough for that also? Should we discuss this, or shall we be amoral when it comes to giving service to our clients?

There is one element in special libraries operation that should be taught somewhere. It is physical appearance. A library can be neat or untidy, attractive or dull. So also can be the library attendants. Virtually nothing has been written to suggest arrangements or color, and, small libraries being the unique places they are, neither architecture, art, nor better homes magazines help. Charles Stevens did write a short piece to stir some thought a few years ago. Entitled "Have You Looked at Your Library Lately?" it suggested a periodic examination to reevaluate arrangements, to notice out-of-date bulletins, to see run-down equipment, messy stacks, dirt; in short, it urged viewing things with the eyes of a newcomer or visitor. But beyond that, the library personnel themselves, in addition to being information experts, are part of the library environment. If the library is attractive in appearance and in effect, the librarians must also support and maintain the attraction. Oh, that some course could include this, with even a bit of charm school added!

Lengthen the Course?

The whole exercise in writing this paper—in considering what is now taught, and in predicting, even to myself, what should be included—leads to one conclusion: library education is suffering from the same proliferation as are libraries themselves. In the case of libraries, we must add more materials on more subjects. In the case of library education, we must offer more subjects by adding more courses. In the case of the librarian, we must acquire more knowledge by taking more courses. But there is not time.

The student bemoans that there isn't enough time for him to take desired electives. The working librarian regrets the lack of that knowledge from the electives which he could not take. The entire profession talks much and often about continuing education, some of which would fill the voids but most of which is intended only to keep us up to date. Library schools are hard pressed to schedule both the fundamentals and the essential techniques of the professionalism of librarianship and still give the students the electives which they want.

The special librarian, upon whom the demands for information can at any time and in any job be so widely varied and so exacting, is apt to feel these deficiencies more acutely than other librarians. Depending upon his time, strength, and initiative, he will attempt to fill the gaps on his own. Librarianship is still a "developing" profession in the United States. The brevity of our required academic period as well as what appears to some persons to be minimal subject coverage does not equate with the years of preparation followed by official certification for the "recognized" professions. Can it ever?

Once upon a time, the requirement for being a librarian was merely local influence—both social and political. Then came training, with a certificate of completion. Education was added, in steps, until 45 years ago a bachelor's degree became the qualifier. As more literacy was needed, 20 years ago the one graduate year was made the standard. Now, as we consider the present inadequacies and future needs of education for librarianship, perhaps it is time to begin thinking about two full years of intellectual study.

Summary

We expect no major changes in special librarianship for the remainder of this century. Technology and literature will continue to proliferate. Company special libraries will expand to keep up with company information needs, and the special librarian will expand his intellectual data base to keep up with the library. More automation will be developed, and some exotic systems will become operational. But special librarianship will continue to be personalized service to a special clientele.

Specifically in education for special librarians, we suggest a continuation of traditional teaching format, formal classes, and the credit and grade system. We urge that the basic professional background courses be continued and emphasized.

A plea has been made for instituting a "pre-library" course of study which could broaden the liberal arts background of library students, add significant subject courses for students of special librarianship, improve the "visibility" of librarianship as a profession, contribute toward recruitment, and positively to undergraduate preparation for the graduate year in library school.

To help the student to educate himself for present and anticipated developments in his company and those affecting his company from outside, we have proposed three courses as being essential to future special librarianship: "Automation Basics," "Business Management for the Special Librarian," and "World Affairs and World Resourses." It is suggested that a substantial library practice program as a requirement toward the MSLS degree would add significantly to the quality of the graduate, to his fine performance on the job, and to his professional development.

At a lower priority level, we have suggested a seminar in "Current Problems in Society" to give the emerging graduate librarian information about the culture in which he will function. This includes background knowledge in subjects which are now or soon will become of possible major importance to special libraries. Subject examples are racial problems, urban blight, and ecology. Of less urgency but still important to the special librarian are three subject units which should be included in existing courses. They are "library nets and network management," "computer subscription services," and "machinery for libraries."

An unanswered question has been posed: "What about the ethics of photocopying?"

The paper closes on the proposition that it may be time to begin thinking about two graduate years of education for librarianship.

FOOTNOTES

[1] John J. Boll, "A Basis for Library Education," *Library Quarterly*, XLII (April 1972), 200.

[2] Jesse H. Shera, "An Educational Program for Special Libraries," in *Libraries and the Organization of Knowledge*, D. J. Foskett, ed. (Hamden, Conn.: Shoe String Press, 1965), p. 181.

[3] Jesse H. Shera, "Dimensions of the Master's Program," in *Libraries and the Organization of Knowledge*, D. J. Foskett, ed. (Hamden, Conn.: Shoe String Press, 1965), p. 168.

[4] Nasser Sharify, "The Need for Change in Present Library Science Curricula," in *Library Education: An International Survey*, Larry Earl Bone, ed. (Champaign, Ill.: Univ. of Illinois Graduate School of Library Science, 1968), p. 180.

[5] Samuel Rothstein, "A Forgotten Issue: Practice Work in American Library Education," in *Library Education: An International Survey*, Larry Earl Bone, ed. (Champaign, Ill.: Univ. of Illinois Graduate School of Library Science, 1968), p. 197.

APPENDIX

A Proposed Curriculum in Library Education

As an active special librarian who is not an educator, it would be presumptuous of me to propose a complete curriculum; undoubtedly there are hidden complexities of which I do not know. Consequently, the lists below contain only those courses that I believe are essential or of major importance.

Core (Required) Courses

Administration of Libraries: Principles of administration, organizational structure, and operation of libraries and information services; leadership, communication, decision making, and control; comparison of administrative situations in different types of libraries.

Introduction to Librarianship: Evolution of the modern library; characteristics and functions of all types of libraries; principles and concepts of library and information science; role of professional associations; current trends in librarianship.

Introductory Cataloging and Classification: Principles and practices in classifying and cataloging library materials; organization of materials, particularly including non-book matter. [Author's comment: If the principles are thoroughly learned, there is no need for in-depth cataloging practice except when the student wants to develop special expertise. The usual "Advanced Cataloging" course is here shown as an elective.]

Library Technical Procedures: Standard operational techniques including acquisitions, circulation, reference and reserve books, serials, interlibrary loans, exchange services, reproduction, maintenance of materials.

Reference Methods: Techniques and materials for finding information; basic reference books; information and materials sources; resolving the question, locating the information source, getting the answer. [Author's comment: Abundant specific sources are good to know "by heart," but better still is the ability to deduce the area categories where certain kinds of information might be found. Instruction and applied practice assignments in this could well replace a heavy memorization program. The course should emphasize where and how to find the sources, no matter what the subject. Less memorization would permit greater general coverage in the practice of techniques.]

For the currently accepted one-year total of graduate work, we would require only two of the remaining "Core" courses.

Government Publications: Acquisition, organization, and use of selected local, national, international, and foreign government publications.
Resources in the Humanities
Resources in Science and Technology
Resources in the Social Sciences

[All three of the above "Resource" courses could be described thusly: Study of standard reference tools in the field; includes books, abstracting journals, and national and commercial information and data centers and their services; pertinent professional societies and their publications; commercial publishers.

Courses for Special Librarianship
Special Libraries: Introduction to purpose and scope of special libraries; administration and structure; relation to sponsoring organization; specialized functions and personal services.
Automation Basics: Fundamentals of systems analysis; flow charting; systems design; computer equipment, uses, and costs; lab. work.
Business Management for the Special Librarian: Economics of profit making; budgeting; purchasing; business records and statistics; communicating with higher management; library personnel; public relations for the library within the organization.

Electives (A Basic List)
Advanced Cataloging
Advanced Reference
Audiovisual Materials and Equipment.
Book Selection
College and University Libraries
Computerized Services and Search Strategy
History of Books and Printing
Information Science
Library Automation
Non-book Materials
The Public Library
The School Library

Comments

As indicated in my paper, I believe in the traditional format in education. While it may not be an attitude popular with "progressive" or liberal educators, I believe that the conventional method has certainly been more educationally complete and effective over the years in producing well-informed, rational, learned persons than have the recent techniques of allowing the ordinary student free choice in what he will or will not study. The old formal ways never inhibited a creative teacher from innovating nor did they repress or crush an interested student or potential scholar.

Much of the expressed dissatisfaction with library school curricula arises from the student attitude that "I know what is best for me." Students may honestly believe this, although very few of them will have any background for determining or evaluating their future needs in a profession in which as yet they have no experience. Obviously, the student cannot wait for extensive experience before choosing his library school courses. I would like to see a capable, well-informed counselor appointed to be available to the student from the beginning of his enrollment. Most important and to the point would be a positive requirement that the student have at least one session with the counselor. The required session could take the form of a one-time seminar limited to approximately 10 persons. If the seminars were scheduled three days per week, and if 10 different students attended each time, a fairly large number could be accommodated during a semester.

The seminar should be free-form, with the aim of helping a student decide what particular area of library work he wished to enter and what courses in the second semester would best prepare him for that field. It would be the responsibility of the counselor to explain adequately the basic content, purpose, and relevance of specific courses. All 10 seminar participants would simultaneously benefit from questions, answers, and discussion.

The seminar would not be expected to result in a complete course outline for each student for the following semester. Rather, it would provide the background information through which he could plan his program. In addition, it would introduce the counselor as an advisor who could be called on for individual help at any time.

If it were possible to lenghten the meeting periods, this type of seminar would provide an excellent forum for discussing specifics of professionalism. Like "the facts of life," professionalism is too often blithely assumed to be known and understood. Unfortunately, the assumption is wrong. We still find young librarians with the forbidding characteristics of autocratic guardians, with little idea of what effective service and satisfaction their education, training, and positions make possible. Of course, it is always difficult to define professionalism exactly. For the present purpose, an overall statement could be: "A committed attitude of dedicated service without restraint." Although this might be open to semantic argument, the service actions which demonstrate it can be discussed.

PART III

ON PROFESSIONAL SCHOOLS

AND CURRICULA

THE FUTURE OF EDUCATION FOR LIBRARY AND INFORMATION SERVICES

Herbert Goldhor

Director
Graduate School of Library Science
University of Illinois

This statement is based on the author's experiences in education for librarianship and his reflections on the past, present, and likely future of this field of endeavor. Time did not permit a systematic review of the literature, let alone the collection of any new data. In addition, the paper is limited essentially to the basic program of preparation for library work, at the master's degree level, and does not encompass the sixth year or doctoral level programs on the one hand, or the undergraduate curriculum in library science or the junior college offerings for library technical assistants, on the other hand. The following discussion relates only to library schools in the United States and Canada, and particularly to the accredited schools. Finally, the time frame for the future is about 20 years at most.

There are two major assumptions to this document. One is that the type of school which is discussed here is and will continue to be a general purpose school—i.e., one which seeks to prepare students for more than one type of library and for more than one type of work. No accredited school has yet made a firm commitment to prepare its students for only one type of library, nor is it likely that any will in the foreseeable future, in view of the fact that librarians can and do move from one type of library to another. In short, this author believes that there is now and probably will continue to be more that is common in the work and problems of different kinds of libraries than is different.

The second main assumption is that the schools for the preparation of librarians must do more than teach students how to perform tasks which are currently being done in libraries, if the schools are to justify their existence and their university connections and if they are to do the best job of which they are capable. The training classes of 50 years ago did exactly this sort of thing, and the narrow vision and inbreeding which resulted should warn us against ever doing it again. It is no doubt true that the poorest schools do not always keep up with the practices of the best libraries, but the goal is clear that the schools should lead the profession and not follow it.

To be more precise, it is assumed that the chief function of the library school is and will continue to be to prepare people for the practice of librarianship, 1) by teaching them what it is that libraries ought to do, in theory, and why, and 2) by acquainting them with a *critical* review of what it is that libraries are presently doing, and why. A young person in library school today can look forward to more than 40 years of practice, or until after 2010 A.D. Even accepting the increasingly important role of continuing education, it is or should be the responsibility of the school to give him the theoretical base for at least half of that period, and not solely to prepare him for his first job.

If this last assumption is not true, we need to question whether university-affiliated library schools are indeed the best or most desirable pattern for preparing future librarians. Presumably it is the validity of this assumption which accounts in large part for the rapid conversion of the British system of education for librarianship, from one which in the past emphasized years of library work experience and at most part-time attendance in organized instruction, to the present which emphasizes full-time attendance at university schools of librarianship.

At intervals, in library periodicals and in state library association meetings, there are scathing attacks on the low quality of library school teaching and on the deadening influence of the library school experience. Library educators could easily present equally devastating reports of the worst of library practice, which is only to say that a profession gets the kind of schools which it deserves. After all, the library school has the student typically for only one year, and in that time cannot be expected to go beyond the technical content of the curriculum to improve or reform his general knowledge, his ability in public speaking, the attractiveness of his personality, or his skill in innovation. If this is accepted, as indeed it must be, then it follows that in such regards the quality of graduates is no higher than the quality of those selected, and the library schools should select "better" students from among the applicants for admission. The simple answer to this is that no one knows how to do that, as will be discussed below.

There can be no doubt that education for librarianship in this country encompasses a range from very good to very poor schools, and that there is generally a great need for improvement. The present writer is far from feeling that library educators face no major problems. However, before this statement proceeds to specific points of the present and future, it will be helpful to take a backward glance at the historical development of library schools. The main impression gained by this writer from such a review is how far we have come and how many right decisions were made. Library schools in this country did drop the teaching of the library hand, and later the requirement that students had to know how to type. The Williamson report of 1923 may not have had quite as pervasive an effect as the Flexner report in 1910 on medical schools, but training classes did convert to university departments, and the qualification for admission generally was raised to completion of the undergraduate bachelor's degree. There are few people now who would regard as a mistake the decision around 1948 to give the master's degree for the first year of library school, in place of the 5th year BSLS. Certainly the doctoral program has earned its way—only one school with such a program for 20 years and then about a dozen more schools in the next 20 years. The creation of organized research agencies within library schools is only about 10 or 12 years old, but there are half a dozen in existence now that are doing work which could hardly have been expected from individual instructors. There are many errors of omission and commission in the history of American library schools, but let us now forget that advances have been made and that the record is not all one-sided.

Size and Organization of Schools

Traditionally, library schools have been small and, in general, this has not been a virtue or an advantage. As of Fall 1971, of 51 accredited schools for which the Committee on Accreditation published data,[1] the mean average number of full-time faculty was 12, the median 12, and the range 5 to 22. The number of master's degrees awarded in 1970/71 averaged 118, with a median of 113 and a range of 24 to 189. The mean average expenditure that year for instructional staff was about $176,000 with a median of $163,500, and a range of $75,700 to over $437,000. These three measures of size are used because they are relatively clear in their definition and relatively consistent in their application.

On the one hand, the accredited schools are getting bigger. For example, in Fall 1964 the average number of full-time faculty in 35 accredited library schools was only seven, and the average expenditures for instructional staff totaled $84,000.[2]

On the other hand, it is probably true that most accredited library schools are the smallest comparable unit on their campuses, by number of staff, amount of budget, square feet of space occupied—but *not* in number of degrees granted. It is recognized that *some* small schools are of high quality, but it is also true that *most* small schools are of low quality.

It is inevitable and desirable that accredited library schools become larger, particularly in number of faculty, so as to be able to allow for subject specialization and for coverage in depth of major areas of instruction. More faculty, better salaries, and more nearly adequate physical quarters are being secured over the long present and will continue to be a high priority need for the future, primarily to enable the schools to do a better job with the present numbers of students and only incidentally—if at all—to handle even larger numbers of students.

Too many university administrators think of a library school as a low budget, low cost operation. Quite apart from the need for better than average library service on the campus, a low cost, low budget library school is likely also to be a low quality operation. We have in recent years experienced a great increase in the number of newly created schools, many of which are too small to be economic or efficient units, let alone high quality units. It would be very desirable if accrediting agencies, foundations, and the U.S. Office of Education could be persuaded not to recognize or aid any university which supports a library school at below a certain minimum level—e.g., a full-time faculty of at least 6 persons, at least 60 master's degrees awarded each year, and an instructional salaries budget (in 1972 dollars) of no less than $90,000—to cut in half the averages reported above.

As far as is known to this writer, no accredited library school is now directly associated with the university library or directly responsible to the librarian—a pattern which once was nearly universal. There are some which are integral parts of the college of education, and this, too, is not a pattern to be emulated. A library school today should have close working relations with the college of education, the department of instructional technology, and the computer laboratory, among others—as well as with the university library—but it should not be an integral part of any one of them. Librarianship is an applied discipline, and over the years new developments may indicate that the library school move into closer rapport with yet some other departments. No trend is discernible, nor is it expected that library schools will be integrated into some other one agency, though probably with the proliferation of more such small and independent units on the campus, an intermediate level administrator may be installed for coordination and control.

Selection of Students

In this writer's opinion, the greatest single problem or challenge of library education is getting an outstanding group of instructors. And the second most difficult and important problem is choosing wisely the students who are to be admitted. No profession can ever hope to have as practitioners only those who are well fitted in personality and aptitude for the work to be done, but it is probably true that librarianship still has more than a few practitioners (i.e., library school graduates) who are temperamentally unsuited to the general ideals of service which we commonly expect of librarians. In part this is because of the situation in the past in which library schools had relatively few applicants and did not often turn down someone who met the formal academic requirements. Fortunately, over the long present most accredited schools have had more qualified applicants than they could accept. If and when the situation changes again, library schools will do the profession a disservice if they fail to screen applicants carefully and to consider their personality critically.

Just what can a library school do to select those who are outgoing, alert, people-oriented, full of life, and interesting to be with? Typically the school asks the candidate to submit three or more letters of reference, and sometimes to have an interview. In over 10 years of experience in reading such letters of reference, this writer cannot recall seeing more than 10 which were critical. Many more tried to convey between the lines a guarded warning or tip, which all too often was not perceived until after the student was admitted and his personality deficiencies experienced first hand. For practical purposes, in this regard the letters of reference are worthless.

The interview is not much better. Ideally, the same person should conduct all the interviews so that he may apply the same criteria and be able to make the necessary comparative judgments. With any large number of applicants, this becomes either a herculean task or a formality. Ideally one would need a psychiatrist to probe beneath the surface which is presented in an interview of, say, 30 to 45 minutes. Even a psychologist to administer and score the MMPI or Rorschach test would be an advance over present practice.

Essentially the problem is that we have to be able to specify what traits we wish in those who are accepted and what traits we are prepared to use as a basis for rejection. The placement officer of every library school sees the end result in sharp contrast; in a period of job shortage, as now, the average intellectual ability of those who get jobs is in general no higher than of those who don't, but what typically characterizes the two groups is the presence or absence of a winning personality. This is a prime area for research; and if librarians don't do it, it is likely never to be done. Douglass and Bryan did some pioneering studies in this regard,[3] but what we need is a standardized test easy to administer and to score—and infallible. By 20 years from now, it is predicted confidently, we will have taken long strides in this direction.

Important as manner and personality are, other things are important, too—e.g., academic achievement and ability. Over the long run, this is being given less and less attention in the selection of students. For one thing, we have learned that grades in college or on the Graduate Record Examination do not correlate very highly with grades in library school—or more importantly with success in the field later. For a second thing, we know that we can take students with a wide span of academic achievement and teach them what they need to know to serve effectively in libraries. For a third thing, grades in college are becoming increasingly homogenized with pass-fail arrangements, lower standards of grading, and other related developments.

For what these opinions may be worth, there are these three positive suggestions which can be made. First, applicants with library work experience (as pages or clerical employees) are usually a good bet, perhaps because they are already a self-selected group. Surely we ought to be able to synthesize the essence of this experience somehow and not make it a requirement for admission to library school. Second, it is desirable and feasible even in the present state of affairs to emphasize the positive in selecting students—e.g., to insist on evidence of leadership in an autobiographical statement and in letters of reference. Third, the old formal requirements for admission are going out of the picture, as they should. Applicants below 35 are not necessarily better candidates than older people. Those without a knowledge of foreign languages are not necessarily less well-prepared for many fields of library work than those with such knowledge. Liberal arts courses are often less relevant than those in engineering, business school, or computer science. In short, it is predicted that, over the long haul, library schools will de-emphasize some of the traditional criteria for admission and sharpen their tools for evaluating the intangible factors.

Curriculum

Strictly speaking, the curriculum consists of all the experiences to which the student is exposed, and the structure or form in which they are organized. Curriculum in this sense does make a difference; surely any library school today is the poorer if it has no course on computers and their possible applications to libraries. But the main impression which this writer has gained from his 16 years of experience in library education is that students learn in spite of the curriculum and not because of it. In part this is because good students will learn much with a poor curriculum, and poor students will learn little with a good curriculum. In part this is because the faculty make the curriculum and not vice versa, and because students learn more (probably) from the faculty as people, and from each other, than they do directly from their courses.

For example, some schools teach reference work by means of case studies, some emphasize the details of specific titles, and some use specific titles only as examples of general types of commonly found reference books. It is this writer's guess that no one of these ways of organizing the course is necessarily superior to the others, and that reference librarians, if tested for their knowledge of sources and for their skill in answering patrons' questions three or five years after graduation from library school, would be ranked in essentially random order insofar as concerns the nature of the reference courses they had in library school. It seems that at best the curriculum can facilitate the learning process, just as at worst it can impede it. But by itself and within broad limits, the curriculum of library schools is far less important than it seems to have been viewed over the long past; and the same trend is evident in colleges generally and other fields of study.

If the curriculum as such is not the most important element, then surely it should be de-emphasized. And over the long present, there has been a steady relaxing of the number of prescribed courses and a corresponding increase in the number of optional or elective courses. In several schools today there is only one required course, called something like "Foundations of Librarianship," and it is predicted that this practice will spread widely in the next decade. After all, students in a graduate library school are adults, and they should be allowed to make their own mistakes instead of being required to make the mistakes prescribed for them by the school.

And if the choice and organization of learning experiences in a formal structure are not that important, how can we best arrange the teaching-learning process? There are undoubtedly many different possible answers to this question, and controlled and reported experimentation with one or another possible pattern would be highly desirable. Just as an example, let us explore the possibilities of a design which rests on the benefits which are frequently found to accrue when a student is permitted to do independent study with an instructor of his choice on a topic of mutual interest. This reduces the formal organization to a minimum, and maximizes the interpersonal relationships between students and instructors. Would it be possible to make this sort of arrangement the norm rather than the exception?

What is being suggested is that, after the foundations course, each student signs up to work for, say, a month with an instructor of his choice (and that is his full course load), and no instructor may have more than, say, 10 or 12 students in any one month (and that is his full teaching load). The group (i.e., both the instructor and the students) then consult together and decide what they will do in that month—perhaps they will take a bus and go visit libraries, perhaps the students will do guided reading, perhaps the instructor will talk to the students about his experiences and ideas, and probably they will decide to use several different approaches in their month together. Notice, however, that there is no subject content stipulated in advance; the instructor and the students study anything they like, without regard to level or possible overlapping with what other groups are doing. Isn't this what happens anyway, in spite of the names of courses? In the golden age of the Graduate Library School of the University of Chicago, with Wilson, Waples, Butler, Joeckel, Randall and Carnovsky, one took courses with the man and it little mattered what was the name of the course he was supposed to be teaching that term.

Perhaps only one further refinement is needed—*viz.*, that every instructor must be continually engaged in some form of research, so that he could always invite his students to join with him in that endeavor if they had no other plan in mind. Would students in such an arrangement profit from a full month of work with Lubetzky, or with Cheney, or with Lowell Martin? There might be grades but surely no examinations. The question arises, however, as to how it will be determined when the student is ready to be graduated. How is that determined now? Typically by the rule of the graduate college that a master's degree candidate must earn "x" number of credit hours to receive the degree. And why this number? It's traditional, it happens to fit the time period of an academic year or of an academic year and a summer, and almost every other school has about the same requirement—so it must be right!

If we were to start from first principles to try to establish a criterion for determining when the student is ready to graduate, one might deduce various possible answers. Let us consider only three. One answer might be that a student graduates when he can pass a comprehensive examination on the content of at least the core of librarianship. Notice that this implies a fixed sequence of courses, for if even half the courses are electives the task of designing a matching comprehensive exam is impossible. Furthermore, there is reason to believe that in the few cases where comprehensive examinations are now used for master's degree candidates, very few people ever fail them finally. (Indeed, it should also be noted that very few students fail to earn the master's degree from accredited library schools for purely academic reasons—certainly no more than 2 percent a year.)

Perhaps a better criterion for determining completion of the master's degree program is whenever the student is judged to be ready to serve effectively in a library at the junior professional level. And just how is this done? Field work as usually performed is for far too short a period of time to make this judgment. Why not arrange it that the degree (Master of Arts or Master of Science) will be awarded not solely upon completion of "x" number of credit hours of courses, but after one full year of work experience in an approved library, with a rating of "satisfactory" from both the work supervisor and a representative of the library school? There are many problems and defects to this but, also, at least three advantages. One is that the student can determine how long he wants to study before he looks for a library which will employ him. A second is that those students who should never have been admitted to library school will probably not even find the necessary year of employment needed to secure the degree. And a third is that the students and the faculty are engaged in a process of working together to prepare the student for his real test of performance in a job.

Here is a third possible logical criterion for deciding when a student is ready to leave the school with his degree. There is great merit in the idea that the only thing we can be sure of is that things will change, and the need consequently is for librarians who are able to adapt to changes yet unknown. If this is so, then perhaps we can give a student his degree whenever he can demonstrate to the faculty (or a faculty committee) a reasoned explanation of two different solutions to each of, say, three major problems in librarianship today. The

115

reason for the two different solutions is that he demonstrate an open mind to various possible approaches.

These are radical ideas which have never been tried, which obviously run counter to all that we have done in the past, and which will cost money and shake up many comfortable patterns now in effect. In other words, the future looks good for them and they (or something like them) will probably be tried somewhere or other and in time become the accepted dogma, and future educators will wonder why it took us so long to see the need for such a change. Clearly, 1) we must decide what we want students to be able to do, when they finish their studies, that they presumably cannot do when they begin those studies, and then 2) we must determine by research what techniques or patterns will work best with what kinds of students to facilitate their learning the necessary skills and knowledge. In that one sentence is wrapped the whole world of educational psychology, and the library educators of the present are only just beginning to move down this road.

The above discussion deals with the most important part of the curriculum, but there are many other aspects of this topic which are relevant and controversial. Only three of these will be treated here, and briefly at that. The bond they have in common derives from the fact that librarianship is an applied rather than a basic discipline, just as engineering and medicine are applied disciplines while physics and the life sciences are basic or pure. An applied discipline is subject to the influence not only of developments in the world of its practitioners, but also of developments in the basic disciplines on which it rests.

What then are the basic disciplines undergirding librarianship? From the point of view of the functions of libraries (as opposed to the nature of their materials), there are four which are most important—*viz.*, education, political science (including public administration), psychology, and sociology. It is hypothesized that a student with a firm command of these four subjects will become a significantly more effective librarian than will a student who knows none of them. If this were tested and found to be true, it would be an important consideration in the selection of library school students. More to the point, however, the library school curriculum should embrace and build on the principles, findings, and factual content of these other disciplines if the relationship is to be a live and vital one. In brief, it is predicted that the course content of library school courses in the future will indeed contain an increasing amount of explicit dependence on these other subjects.

By much the same token, there are courses in other departments of any university which are relevant to the concerns of librarians and which should be available to and taken by library school students. Presumably this was one of the main reasons for moving the preparation of librarians into the university—to secure the benefits of intellectual cross-fertilization. With a few conspicuous exceptions, most library schools might as well be on a desert island as far as concerns the intellectual cross-fertilization of master's degree students. Most library schools cross-list very few courses, some don't even allow their students to take courses in other departments and count them toward the degree, few have any faculty members who are not pure librarians, and most presume to teach their students the elements of administration, statistical methods, computer programming, audiovisual media, the role and effects of mass media, etc. Admittedly, students find it easier to study any such subject when it is presented in the context of examples, terminology, assumptions, and practices of libraries, but the major advances in those fields are not coming from librarians but from those who devote themselves full time to research and teaching of the subject in question. The pattern for the future is clear; library schools will use the resources of other departments much more than has been true up until now.

On a level of even deeper involvement, librarianship is now and will surely continue to be a growing and developing field of study. Inevitably its sphere of interest intersects with that of some other closely related but different fields—e.g., at present, information science and instructional technology. The question arises whether the library school should attempt to incorporate the other field into itself. In general, this writer thinks it would be best not to seek to do that, but to establish a close working relationship of equals. Usually the other discipline has some (or more) independent non-library roots and applications, and it will develop best by being free to grow in any direction which seems indicated. In the same vein, it would be undesirable for the library school to be subsumed under the other subject field and to be expected to grow and develop primarily along those lines. Furthermore, library schools would do well to be free to form similar working alliances with yet other subject fields in the future, as technology or other forces make for changes in our concerns. The hallmark of a live and vital field of study is not that it absorbs and dominates new and related disciplines but rather that it shows the results of integrating within itself the appropriate theories, techniques, and findings of those disciplines. The only thing we can be sure of is that things will change.

Teaching Methods

Teaching method is primarily a dimension of the instructor. One person can lecture incisively and effectively, while another stumbles and makes a mess. But there are some generalizations which can be essayed. It seems reasonably clear that learning will be maximized when the teaching process is individualized. One of the great developments which even now makes this feasible is computer-assisted instruction (CAI). While educational television goes ruthlessly on, regardless of the attention (or lack of attention) of the students, CAI comes to a grinding halt whenever the student fails to interact. Even now there are several CAI applications in library schools, and the potential for this technique in the teaching of library science is as great as for any subject. The computer record of each student's response to each question in the program gives the instructor a hitherto unequalled opportunity to follow his thinking, and to see just where and when he missed the point.

Other related but different techniques for individualized instruction include the auto-tutorial method and Keller's Proctorial System of Instruction.[4] The former emphasizes the use of various media as appropriate to the content, in a learning carrel, while the instructor, the person who plans the grand strategy, is also available for questions. The long-term result is likely to be the displacement of the classroom but not of the instructor. The latter is a system for breaking up a course into small units and allowing each student to go at his own pace, while requiring success in the end-of-unit examination before going on; lectures are used for motivation rather than as sources of information, and graduate assistants are readily available for consultation. One can only hope and believe that library schools too will adopt and use the best of these devices.

The point is that teaching can be improved, that there are many new and exciting techniques and approaches, and that student learning is more important than "covering the subject." Using behavioral objectives is one way to guarantee that the emphasis will be put where it belongs.[5] The younger generation of library school instructors, in this writer's opinion, is on the whole better prepared in terms of educational psychology and teaching methods than is the older generation; it is to be hoped that the next generation will be even better.

Faculty

As stated above, the single most important factor in the success (or failure) of any school is the faculty. Both quantity and quality are important. There should be enough instructors to 1) allow for some reasonable degree of specialization, and 2) hold down the ratio of students to faculty. Graduate education in America in the best departments usually involves a ratio of about 7.5 students to each instructor; in most accredited library schools today the ratio is at least twice that high. But the best schools have lower ratios, and it is certainly desirable—and expected—that the average ratio of students to faculty improve in the years ahead. In 20 years, it is predicted, the ratio will be about 10 to 1 in most schools.

Important as the number of instructors is, far more important and difficult is the matter of quality. For one thing, it is easy to see that the percentage of library school instructors with the earned doctorate has been steadily rising over the last 20 years and will undoubtedly continue to rise in the next two decades. It is predicted that by 1992, almost all full-time instructors in accredited library schools will have a doctor's degree. And in general this will be a good thing. There will always be a place for the unusual individual who is self-taught or has gotten maximum mileage from his work experience—remember George Lyman Kittredge in English and at Harvard ("Who could examine me?").

For a second thing, there will be a steady diminution of emphasis on practical work experience in libraries, though by the same token some such experience (say five years or so) is essential for teaching an applied discipline. The point is that there will be an ever greater emphasis on theory, research, and the ability to analyze critically the problems which libraries face and the solutions which they employ. The relative contributions of graduate study and of work experience to the preparation of instructors has already long been shifting from the latter to the former and will surely continue to do so, as our world and this profession get more complicated.

In the third place, it is confidently predicted that library school faculty will inevitably be more active in research in the years ahead than they are now. One reason for this is that we will need to know more about the true relationships between people and books (and the organized collections of books we call libraries). And the single most important group of people for ascertaining these truths is—and will be—the faculty of the graduate library schools. A second reason is that in general the person who does research on a continuing basis is a better instructor because of that. Research and teaching are not opposites, but are complementary halves of the profound urge to learn the truth and to convey it to others. Given a certain minimum experience as a working librarian (say, between finishing the M.S. degree program and beginning the Ph.D.), it is far preferable that a library school instructor have an ongoing research program than more and more years of practical experience. It is for this reason that mature library administrators will find it increasingly more difficult to get positions as library school faculty.

There are many other additional and intangible aspects of quality to be desired of instructors—e.g., personality, ability to adapt to changing circumstances, an interest in assisting the members of the next generation to become even better than oneself, a willingness to keep learning, etc. These cannot be easily gauged in advance or correctly assessed after even a few years of teaching experience. Like the rest of higher education, library schools are going to be tougher in the future than they have been in the past in evaluating the quality of an instructor's worth, in denying him tenure if there is even reasonable doubt that he deserves it, and in modifying the principles of tenure so that it may not be used to protect the inefficient.

Research in Education for Librarianship

At various points in the above statement, attention was called to the need for research—not only to ascertain the truths of librarianship but specifically with reference to education for librarianship. There are assumptions, both implicit and explicit, in our practices, there are myths and hallowed traditions, there are conventions, and there are administrative and curricular arrangements which are practical responses to specific problems. But the chances are that they range from being wholly false to largely true, and the only sure way we have to find which are false and which are true is the scientific method.

As things stand now, we don't even have a regular compilation of meaningful statistics. We have very few analyses of the current facts concerning and arising out of a given practice. We have even fewer experimental studies in any aspect of library education. Almost all the research in librarianship to date has been two-dimensional, when there is every reason to believe that, especially in education, we need to treat several variables simultaneously. For all these reasons it is predicted that research in education for librarianship will increase steadily in the next 20 years. By then there will be at least one center for research in library education.

This is not really as novel or as difficult as it might seem. Most schools are continually seeking to improve themselves, but few make a study of their efforts and report the results. No accredited library school should be allowed to continue to be accredited unless it conducts at least one experiment every five years. It doesn't matter whether the experiment succeeds or fails; what matters is that the experience be recorded, that appropriate observations be collected, and that the whole record be made available to other schools.

Cooperation Between Library Schools

Of the many other possible topics which might be discussed concerning the present and possible future operation of library schools, the present writer finds one to be of major importance—the need for and potential benefits of cooperation between library schools. Typically in the past—and in the present—each library school has acted independently and without regard to other schools, whether the question is overlapping and duplication or gaps between schools. Cooperation between library schools (as between libraries) costs money; so does the lack of cooperation, but we are already used to the dollar costs of lack of cooperation. The one sharpest urge to cooperation is the offer of funds for that purpose or, conversely, the threat of reduced funds by an agency with authority over two or more schools—e.g., a state board of higher education. It would seem likely that in the foreseeable future there will be more and more federal funds available for inter-institutional cooperation and joint planning, and that there will be mounting pressures (particularly on publicly supported institutions) to consider realistically and imaginatively the existence and resources of all comparable institutions in a given region.

Another hard-learned principle of academic cooperation is that no one department can move faster than is permitted by the announced goals or policies of its overhead institution. That is to say, colleges and universities in a given region need to establish a firm basis of specialization, before their respective library schools can really come down to specifics. And this has been notoriously hard for almost any two institutions to do. The next 20 years, however, promise to be hard ones indeed for higher education, and if boards of trustees and presidents cannot agree on even approximate areas of cooperation and coordination, other agencies, like state legislatures, may have to knock heads together.

Library schools would do well to begin to explore what they can do better together than separately. Regular meetings of the schools' administrators and instructors would be a small but necessary beginning step. Few persons in any given school are really well informed on the policies and practices of any other school. Certainly there is no excuse for two schools in the same region offering the same specialized course in the same summer—as has happened. New technology also offers new opportunities for such cooperation; perhaps one school can do computer programming for two schools, while the other handles educational television for both.

There has been a sharp rise in the number of academic consortia over the last 10 years, and presumably this device will continue to be used widely in the years ahead. Universities everywhere in this country are increasingly stressing the spirit of the situation and brushing away the traditional formalities that have preserved the letter. As far as can be learned, library schools today have much more freedom to act than they have yet used, and they will not be able to blame any failure to act on the intransigence of their parent bodies.

Final Remarks

This statement has emphasized some of the many changes likely to take place in the next 20 years. But there are some important values which will certainly continue to be important—e.g., the eagerness of the young to learn, and their willingness to consider new and radical ideas; the thrill that comes to the instructor when he perceives that the student has grasped a concept and now understands it; and the satisfaction that comes from seeing graduates on the job meet and solve library science problems.

FOOTNOTES

[1] ALA Committee on Accreditation, *Statistical Data from Annual Review Reports, 1970-71* (March 1972).

[2] Sarah R. Reed, *Students, Faculty, Funds—1966 vs. 1964* (U.S. Office of Education, n.d.). (Multilithed.)

[3] Robert R. Douglass, "Personality of the Librarian" (unpublished Ph.D. thesis, University of Chicago Graduate Library School, 1957); and Alice I. Bryan, *The Public Librarian: A Report of the Public Library Inquiry* (Columbia University Press, 1952).

[4] Fred S. Keller, "Good-Bye, Teacher. . .'," *Journal of Applied Behavior Analysis*, I (1968), 78-89.

[5] Robert F. Mager, *Preparing Instructional Objectives* (Palo Alto, Calif.: Fearon Publishers, 1962).

INFORMATION SCIENCE:
ITS PLACE IN
THE LIBRARY SCHOOL
CURRICULUM

F. Wilfrid Lancaster

Professor
Graduate School of Library Science
University of Illinois

A brief glance at the catalog of any major library school in the United States will indicate some concern for "information science." Course offerings include such titles as "introduction to information science," "information storage and retrieval," "specialized information centers," "information systems theory," "systems analysis," "evaluation of information systems," and "library mechanization." Some schools already call themselves schools of library and information science or schools of library and information services. It may not be altogether clear, however, just what "information science" is, how "information science" relates to "library science," how much "information science" should be included within the curricula of graduate schools of library science, and how the "information science" component should be integrated with the rest of the curriculum. It is these questions that we intend to investigate further in this paper.

Information Science

Perhaps one of the best definitions of information science appeared in 1962 in the *Proceedings of the Conference on Training Science Information Specialists.*[1] According to this definition, information science is:

> The science that investigates the properties and behavior of information, the forces governing the flow of information, and the means of processing information for optimum accessibility and usability. The processes include the origination, dissemination, collection, organization, storage, retrieval, interpretation and use of information. The field is derived from or related to mathematics, logic, linguistics, psychology, computer technology, operations research, the graphic arts, communications, library science, management, and some other fields.

According to the same source, an "information scientist" is: "one who studies and develops the science of information storage and retrieval, who

122

devises new approaches to the information problem, who is interested in information in and of itself."

If we accept these definitions, we could look upon library science as a branch of information science and upon a librarian as one species of information scientist.

However, it may be more accurate to regard librarianship and information science as two areas that impinge one on another. Librarianship impinges on many other areas. For example, the subject of "library administration" represents the intersection of librarianship with the broad field of management science, while "library buildings" represents the intersection of librarianship with architecture and design. But library science is much closer to information science than it is to these other fields. In fact, if we represented these various areas by overlapping circles we would probably recognize a considerable overlap between librarianship and information science, whereas the overlap between librarianship and the other fields would be quite slight.

A library is one type of information storage and retrieval system. There are others, including airline reservation systems, command and control systems, management information systems, crime detection systems, and systems for medical diagnosis. The librarian is primarily concerned with one particularly important medium of information transfer, the printed document; and librarianship has traditionally involved the collection, organization, storage, retrieval and dissemination of these documents—in other words, librarians are intimately concerned with *documentation*.

The major steps in the documentary information transfer process are well displayed in Figure 1, adapted from King and Bryant.[2] Librarians should be

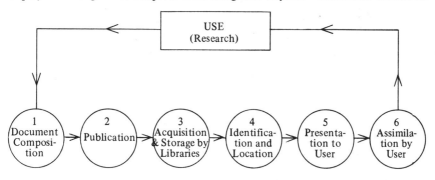

Figure 1

interested in all of the activities illustrated here, although they are most concerned with the acquisition and storage of documents, their identification and location (including cataloging, indexing, abstracting, classification and searching processes) and their physical presentation to potential users.

It can be seen, from the previously cited definition that information science is very broad in scope and that, besides librarians, many other professionals are involved in information transfer activities, including the activities we have referred to as *documentation*. The scope of information science is well illustrated by an examination of several issues of the *Journal of the American*

Society for Information Science or the volumes of the *Annual Review of Information Science and Technology.*

Most of the other facets of information science impinge in some way upon library science. Also, many of the most important developments in information science in the last 30 years are attributable to people—chemists, mathematicians, computer specialists, and others—who are not librarians. It seems, then, that library science cannot be taught in isolation but must be related to various other aspects of the field of information science. What these other aspects are, and how they relate to librarianship, will be investigated below.

The Content of Information Science Education

Many different academic programs in information science now exist in the United States, some in library schools and some not. Offering great variety, they are variously derived from such fields as library science, linguistics, computer science, systems engineering, and business data processing. Borko and Hayes[3] have identified at least four different orientations in information science curricula:

1. *Theoretically oriented.* In these curricula, outside the library school, information science is viewed as a distinct discipline with its own methodology and research interest. Emphasis is on theory and courses are generally drawn from mathematics, logic, and perhaps linguistics and behavioral science (communication). Courses in hardware, programming, and data base management are included.

The library is viewed as one possible target of information science techniques. However, these programs generally do not emphasize practical applications of information science. Information science programs of this type have been developed at Ohio State[4] and at the University of Dayton. The Dayton program, as described by Debons and Otten,[5] is interdisciplinary in nature, its core being based upon the fields of behavioral science, computer science, engineering, and basic sciences.

2. *Computer-science oriented.* In this situation "information science" is regarded as equivalent to or subsidiary to computer science, the primary emphasis being the computer itself. Frequently, such programs are located in engineering schools. They tend to stress the mathematics and logic involved in computer hardware and software design. Applications discussed are frequently oriented toward engineering or mathematics, but may include applications to other problems, including information retrieval, linguistics, neuroanatomy, and public health. The University of North Carolina, Department of Computer and Information Science, presents an example of a curriculum of this type.

3. *Library oriented.* These information science curricula are offered within a library school. They equate information science with documentation. The emphasis is on the use of computers in libraries, including automation of technical processes as well as various facets of information retrieval and dissemination.

4. *Systems oriented.* These curricula deal largely with the methodology of systems analysis. Specifically emphasized are analysis and design of information systems and networks, including libraries. Management and decision-making

124

aspects, rather than operational and service needs, are stressed. The MS in Information Science offered by the School of Library Service, UCLA, is based upon a curriculum of this type.[6]

Information Science in the Library School

Clearly, there is a limit to the legitimate scope of information science within the library school curriculum. The "theoretically oriented" curriculum would be out of place, although students in library school should certainly receive some theory—for example, indexing and classification theory. The computer-science orientation is equally out of place, although students should be made familiar with the capabilities of computers, particularly their capabilities for handling bibliographic records. The orientations numbered 3 and 4 above (library oriented and systems oriented) appear much more appropriate from the viewpoint of structuring a library school curriculum in this area.

We clarify the role of information science in the library school curriculum if we regard information science as providing a discipline or series of tools applicable to library problems. Giuliano[7] has proposed that the relationship between information science and librarianship is that between a science on the one hand and a profession on the other. What we should be concerned with is *the information science education of the librarian*. Giuliano suggests that the relationship between information science and librarianship is very similar to the relationship between medical research and medicine. Unfortunately, according to Giuliano, librarianship has in the past been concerned almost exclusively with the library as an institution. This is analogous to regarding medicine as equivalent to "hospitals" and to basing medical education on the hospital as an institution. We must get away from our present "institutional" approach to library education and devote more time and effort to instructing students in methods of information transfer in general. Giuliano goes on to emphasize this point as follows:

> I would like to suggest a rather different definition for librarianship in the future, one which does not depend upon working within a certain type of institution but which is based on professional activities dealing with knowledge transfer. The professional "bag" of the librarian should be knowledge transfer just as the professional "bag" of an M.D. should be preventing disease and curing people. The knowledge transfer function encompasses those procedures necessary and appropriate for the assembling of knowledge, its systematic organization, its restructuring and representation, its storage, its retrieval and dissemination. These are, of course, the traditional functions of librarianship, but librarianship as it has been taught traditionally has been concerned with the application of only a narrow collection of highly institutionalized technologies and procedures for carrying these functions through. Many new techniques and procedures exist today, and many others are in the research and development stages.

> Information science comprises the set of research and development undertakings necessary to support the profession of librarianship. Just

as a medical scientist need not be a medical practitioner, an information scientist need not be a librarian. An M.D. may do research in a hospital and a librarian may do research in a library, but non-M.D.'s may do medical research and nonlibrarians may do information science research.

Susan Artandi[8] stresses the importance of information science in the library school curriculum on the following grounds:

> Librarians today are expected to set up and operate computer-based book catalogs, Selective Dissemination of Information Systems, and data banks. They are engaged in the construction of thesauri and the design and operation of computer-based circulation, acquisition, or serial control systems. They are called upon to set up systems which are to achieve certain objectives at a certain cost, to evaluate their own operations, and to suggest and justify changes relative to the new technology. There is also an increase in respectable library-related research, and practically all of this research requires knowledge of methods for obtaining, analyzing, processing, and evaluating data as well as the ability to judge how and when computers can aid these processes.

In actual fact, while the library school curriculum should not be concerned with the training of information scientists in the broad sense, it should certainly be concerned with:

1) Providing all students with at least an introduction to those aspects of information science that impinge most significantly upon library science—i.e., those techniques from information science that can be expected to be most valuable to the librarian in providing efficient, viable library services, whatever the type of library.

2) Providing a core of information science offerings to allow a student, if he wishes, to obtain a degree in library science with a specialization in information science. Students with this type of orientation would be prepared to take up specialized positions in general libraries (e.g., library automation positions in university or college libraries), or to take up positions in specialized information centers operated by universities, government agencies or industrial organizations, where the dynamic information service offered may require a knowledge of techniques of document storage, organization, retrieval and dissemination beyond the level needed by the librarian functioning in a more traditional, relatively passive library environment.

With these two aims in view, it is appropriate to consider what should be the content of information science instruction within the library school. I feel that information science impinges upon librarianship most in the following areas:

1) Application of modern technology to library problems. This includes automation of technical processes in libraries, reprography and facsimile transmission, networking, use of telecommunications in general, and fundamentals of computers and computer programming.

2) Application of scientific methodologies to library problems. This includes systems analysis and relevant techniques from management sciences,

industrial engineering, and operations research. Cost-effectiveness analysis and PPBS techniques might be included here.

3) Current approaches to the design and implementation of information services. This includes modern methods of information storage, retrieval and dissemination, including equipment considerations, indexing and abstracting, construction and use of controlled vocabularies, searching techniques, studies of users and user needs, and evaluation of information services.

Despite the stringent criticisms of Ellsworth Mason,[9, 10] among others, it seems clear that libraries will become increasingly automated in the future. Computers are now being used routinely in many libraries in such activities as ordering and acquisition, serials control, cataloging, production of catalog cards and printed catalogs, and circulation control. The on-line library catalog appears to be on the horizon. Atkinson[11] has already indicated that, in the not-too-far-distant future, no further cards will be filed in the card catalog of the Ohio State University Libraries.

While most of this activity has, as might be expected, occurred in the relatively large university libraries, it is by no means restricted to these giants. Interesting and innovative automation projects exist in a number of smaller institutions, including public libraries, college libraries, and the libraries of public school systems. Computer costs contribute to decline, while labor costs continue to rise. It seems very likely, then, that the move toward automation of library processes will continue, at accelerated pace, in the future. An added impetus to these activities is provided by the increasing realization that, while not all libraries have funds available to allow the development of automated procedures, inter-institutional cooperation at national, state or local levels makes certain automated procedures both feasible and economical.

Modern telecommunications technology, coupled with the increasing availability of important bibliographic data bases in machine-readable form, now makes it possible for us to implement viable library networks for the exploitation and interchange of bibliographic data. Excellent examples are the Biomedical Communication Network of the State University of New York and the network of libraries linked by the Ohio College Library Center. While these operations are now restricted to machine-readable data, it is likely that future developments will allow library networks to expand to permit facsimile transmission and/or the remote viewing of microform images selected from a random-access store located in a library many miles from the viewing station.

Not all students leaving library school will find themselves involved in the design and implementation of automated systems, but some will, and the number of positions available in the area of library automation will certainly increase. For these positions we will need librarians who have been trained in techniques of systems analysis and design, who understand the capabilities and limitations of computers and associated telecommunications devices, and who have enough programming background to be able to communicate intelligently with professional programmers.

Many of our present students may never be involved directly in the design and implementation of automated systems. However, they will almost certainly have to adapt to work in an automated environment, if not immediately, then at some future date. Some will eventually find themselves in management positions involving automated operations. All students must at least be trained to understand the general functions and capabilities of machine-based systems. Above all, library school education must stress the need for flexibility and breadth of vision in order that the future librarian can adapt to the changing situations and conditions that future technology will undoubtedly bring, but which we are unable to predict in detail at the present time.

A second group of techniques, which represents a close common interest between librarianship and information science and which is of direct concern to the practising librarian, related to the "scientific management" of libraries. In the past, library management has been more of an art than a science and many library managers have performed remarkably well on the basis of intuitive and seat-of-the-pants approaches. However, libraries, especially the great academic libraries, continue to grow and to become increasingly demanding, but in terms of space and financial resources. In some quarters, at least, there is a strong feeling that these libraries are rapidly approaching a crisis and that, especially in these days of economic stringency, they can no longer be allowed to grow unchecked. Librarians appear to be becoming increasingly interested in techniques from business administration, industrial engineering and operations research that are applicable to resource allocation and the optimum utilization of library budgets. Such techniques include cost-effectiveness and cost-benefit analysis and Planning, Programming and Budgeting System (PPBS) procedures. Also relevant are operations research and mathematical modeling procedures that can be used to predict probable future use patterns, including circulation demand, the number of copies of items required, and mean loan periods, and which are thus applicable to policies for purchase and retirement of library materials. Excellent examples of applicable procedures have been presented in a textbook by Morse,[12] in the work of Leimkuhler at Purdue University, and in a series of reports from the University of Lancaster in England.

A closely related problem is that of evaluation of library service. It is only in the last decade that serious attention has been devoted to methodologies that may be used in the objective evaluation of various library activities. A good example is the document delivery test devised by Orr *et al.*[13] to evaluate the document delivery capabilities of medical libraries.

The library school student is unlikely to become a specialist in operations research or industrial engineering. Nevertheless, the principles of scientific management are obviously of great importance and the student must be made aware of the techniques that exist in other fields and that may be applicable to library problems. Relevant course offerings should be available in the library school, perhaps developed in association with other departments of the university.

Finally, we turn to the broad area of information storage and retrieval, which is perhaps the heart of information science as it affects the librarian. While librarians have been concerned with information retrieval for centuries, traditional approaches to storage, retrieval and dissemination problems have tended to break down. Many new approaches to these problems have been developed in the past 25 years, mostly from outside the library profession. Only a decade ago, the librarian was concerned almost exclusively with printed books and journals and with printed indexes to these. He can no longer so restrict himself.

Computer-based retrieval systems are still only in their infancy but they are obviously here to stay, and they will multiply and become of increasing importance. The growing availability of machine-readable data bases, coupled with advances in on-line computer technology, has greatly extended the accessibility and impact of such systems. The reference librarian of the future may use an on-line computer terminal more than he will use traditional printed tools. The on-line terminal will provide access to the resources of his own library, because the library catalog itself will be on-line, and it will also provide access to virtually unlimited bibliographic resources in other institutions. Already the reference librarian in a medical library must be able to search on a MEDLINE terminal in order to exploit most effectively the vast resources of the National Library of Medicine. This is just the beginning.

It is quite obvious that more and more bibliographic data bases will soon be available for on-line, remote interrogation. Such data bases will include general data bases (e.g., covering the whole of medicine) and specialized data bases (e.g., covering neurology or diabetes). While medical libraries have taken the lead in making bibliographic resources available on-line, it is certain that on-line systems will soon extend widely into other fields. As computer and terminal costs come down, and as communications costs are drastically reduced by improved communications and time-sharing networks, the on-line terminal will become increasingly an everyday tool of the reference librarian, providing access not only to document representations but also, eventually, to the full text of documents themselves.

In order to exploit these systems most effectively, librarians will need to understand indexing principles and policies, the structure of vocabularies used for indexing, and fundamentals of searching strategy. They will also need a considerable knowledge of the information resources of the United States, including the many specialized information centers and services that now exist. In addition, librarians should be able to evaluate the various services and to determine which are likely to be of greatest value to the particular user population to be served. They will need some knowledge of techniques of evaluation and procedures that can be applied to studies of user needs for information services.

Those librarians who will work with the producers of information services (e.g., government agencies, professional societies, industrial and commercial organizations) will, of course, need to know much more about techniques of storage, retrieval, and dissemination than the librarians who are merely users of these services.

Integration of Information Science into the Curriculum

Having discussed the broad areas of information science that appear to have greatest relevance to librarianship and the education of librarians, it is appropriate to give some consideration to how information science should be integrated into the library school curriculum. Is the subject matter covered in a special group of courses that are separate from the other, more traditional courses, or is it completely integrated in the curriculum so that information science techniques and philosophies permeate virtually all areas of library instruction?

Artandi[14] expressed the opinion that information science must pervade the curriculum of the library school:

> I would like to suggest strongly that to take care of the needs of library school students it is not enough to append a few courses to the tail-end of existing curricula. A much more imaginative and a much more fundamental approach is needed. The new point of view and the research findings of information science are relevant to all courses and should be integrated into the entire curriculum. This will make library school curricula not only more up-to-date but also more exciting and meaningful.

A similar opinion was expressed by Swank:[15]

> There are three ways of relating the newer content of documentation and information science to the older content of librarianship. First is the addition of specialized courses to the existing curriculum, as many schools are now doing. This is useful and expedient, but achieves no basic integration. The old curriculum remains substantially untouched. Second is the offering of separate new curricula in information science that are parallel or alternative to the old curriculum, as a few library schools and the separate schools of information science are now doing. This approach not only fails of integration but actually emphasizes the apparent dichotomy between the new and the old. The third way, to which I subscribe, is the blending of the new content into a basically revised version of the old curriculum—or, if the converse pleases more, the blending of the old content into a basically new curriculum.
>
> I prefer the integrated approach because I do not believe that information science is a field separate from librarianship. It is rather a fresh insight into the nature of librarianship. The processes of collection building, organization, and utilization are, for example, common to all library and information systems.

If we regard information science as a tool of librarians (or librarianship as one application of information science), the "integrated approach" is justified and "information science" concepts should appear in many of the courses taught within the library school. Information science impinges on all the major library activities depicted in Figure 1 (p. 123), and should be treated in the curriculum accordingly. For example, the introduction to scientific management principles should be integrated into courses on library administration, while cataloging courses should certainly concern themselves with the use of the computer in cataloging activities, including the production of book catalogs and catalog cards, the exploitation of MARC tapes, and the implications of the on-line catalog.

Nevertheless, certain areas of information science do not easily integrate completely into the traditional library curriculum. Information storage and retrieval, for example, is a subject that deserves to stand on its own and to have several courses, basic and advanced, devoted to it. Library automation may be regarded in the same way for, while the application of computers to cataloging

130

may legitimately be integrated into the cataloging curriculum, it is not clear where in the curriculum various other computer applications would be treated (e.g., circulation systems and serials control systems). Moreover, a full appreciation of any automated system requires some basic understanding of systems analysis procedures, programming, coding, and equipment capabilities that are common to library automation in general and therefore best treated in a single course.

There is a further consideration. We have spoken of the need to allow students to obtain a degree in library science with a specialization in information science. Obviously, then, we must provide a program of courses to allow such a specialization. While certain aspects of information science may be integrated completely into the curriculum, a subcurriculum in information science must exist within the library school. To detail the specific courses in such a subcurriculum is outside the scope of this paper, although I have indicated the general areas upon which we probably need to concentrate in the information science education of the librarian.

Although it may not be possible to fully integrate the subject matter into the library school curriculum, it certainly seems desirable that *all* students be exposed to some minimum level of information science. Some introductory course should be required of all students and should perhaps be integrated with the general introductory course on librarianship that is a prerequisite to other library science courses in many schools.

Levels of Information Science Education

The library school must provide information science education at various levels. At the master's level, both basic and advanced courses must be available, and the capability should exist for doctoral level research in the general area of information transfer processes. It is possible that the library school should also concern itself with service courses for other departments of the university. Such courses would survey the information resources available in a particular discipline and how those resources may be exploited most effectively (i.e., this level of education would be directed at the *user* of information services rather than at the information specialist).

Debons and Otten[16] have discussed the need for information science education at undergraduate, predoctoral (master's) and doctoral levels. At the undergraduate level, the aim should be to produce information technologists, whereas at the master's level the training should be designed to prepare individuals to function as information systems specialists (i.e., individuals capable of assisting in the "maximization of data utilization"). At the doctoral level, the purpose of the training is to enable the individual to be an "information scholar" or "informatologist." At this level, courses and research prepare the individual to conduct the experiments in information transfer and information utilization. The "informatologist" is concerned with developing principles, theories and laws about information and operations on information. He is also, presumably, involved in the education of future information specialists.

Conclusion

In many ways libraries have changed remarkably little, in their services and operations, in the last century. It is almost certain that this period of comparative stability is over and that the "library of the future" may be considerably different from the traditional library we have become accustomed to. We cannot predict exactly what this library of the future will look like, although we can foresee certain probable, broad trends. It is clear that the next 25 years are likely to be extremely exciting technologically. We are just beginning to scratch the surface of the possibilities for applying technological advances to problems of information transfer. Rapid developments are taking place in such activities as computer-aided instruction, networking, on-line computer technology, microform technology, cable television, mass digital storage, machine processing of text, and publishing and distribution methods. Some of these developments, collectively, may result in significant overall improvements in future methods of information handling. Librarianship will be greatly affected by these developments. Libraries will be entering a period of great change and the curricula of our library schools must reflect this. Above all else, we must educate librarians capable of adapting to the changes that new technologies will inevitably bring.

FOOTNOTES

[1] Georgia Institute of Technology, *Proceedings of the Conference on Training Science Information Specialists* (Atlanta, Ga., 1962).

[2] D. W. King and E. C. Bryant, *The Evaluation of Information Services and Products* (Washington D.C.: Information Resources Press, 1971).

[3] H. Borko and R. Hayes, *Education for Information Science (Documentation)* (Los Angeles: Univ. of California, Institute of Library Research, 1970).

[4] M. C. Yovits, "Information Science: Toward the Development of a True Scientific Discipline," *American Documentation*, XX, No. 4 (October 1969), 369-76.

[5] A. Debons and K. Otten, "Foundations of a Concept for an Education Program in Information Science," *American Documentation*, XX, No. 4 (October 1969), 346-51.

[6] Borko and Hayes, *Education for Information Science.*

[7] V. E. Giuliano, "The Relationship of Information Science to Librarianship—Problems and Scientific Training," *American Documentation*, XX, No. 4 (October 1969), 344-45.

[8] S. Artandi, "The Relevance of Information Science to Library School Curricula," *American Documentation*, XX, No. 4 (October 1969), 337-38.

[9] E. G. Mason, "Computers in Libraries," *Library Resources and Technical Services*, XVI (Winter 1972), 5-10.

[10] Mason, "Automation? Or Russian Roulette?" *Proceedings of the 1972*

Clinic on Library Applications of Data Processing, ed. by F. W. Lancaster (Urbana: Univ. of Illinois, Graduate School of Library Science, 1972).

[11] H. C. Atkinson, Remarks made at the Ninth Annual Clinic on Library Applications of Data Processing, Urbana, April 1972.

[12] P. M. Morse, *Library Effectiveness: A Systems Approach* (Cambridge, Mass.: M.I.T. Press, 1968).

[13] R. H. Orr, *et al.*, "Development of Methodologic Tools for Planning and Managing Library Services," *Bulletin of the Medical Library Association*, XXVI, No. 3 (July 1968), 235-67; No. 4 (October 1968), 380-403.

[14] Artandi, "The Relevance of Information Science."

[15] R. C. Swank, "Documentation and Information Science in the Core Library School Curriculum," *Special Libraries*, January 1967, 40-44.

[16] Debons and Otten, "Foundations."

BIBLIOGRAPHY

Bracken, M. C. and C. W. Shilling. *Education and Training of Information Specialists in the U.S.A.* (Washington, D.C.: George Washington University, Biological Sciences Communication Project, 1966).

————— . *Survey of Practical Training in Information Science* (Washington, D.C.: George Washington University, Biological Sciences Communication Project, 1967).

Federation Internationale de Documentation. *International Conference on Education for Scientific Information Work*. (The Hauge: F.I.D., September 1967).

Goldwyn, A. J. and A. M. Rees. *The Education of Science Information Personnel—1964: Proceedings of an Invitational Conference*. (Cleveland, Ohio: Western Reserve University, 1965).

Hayes, R. H. "Education in Information Science," *American Documentation*, XX, No. 4 (October 1969), 362-65.

Hayes, R. M. "Information Science in Librarianship," *Libri*, XIX, No. 3 (1969), 216-36.

Heilprin, L. B., B. E. Markuson, and F. L. Goodman, eds. *Proceedings of the Symposium on Education for Information Science*, Warrenton, Va., September 7-10, 1965 (Washington, D.C.: Spartan Books, 1965).

Hillman, D. J. "How to Win the Pentathlon—Unifying Theories of Information Science," *American Documentation*, XX, No. 4 (October 1969), 335-36.

Hoyt, R. H. "An Analysis of Information Science Programs," *American Documentation*, XX, No. 4 (October 1969), 358-61.

Klempner, I. M. "Information Science Unlimited? ... a Position Paper," *American Documentation*, XX, No. 4 (October 1969), 339-43.

Rees, A. M. and D. Riccio. "Curriculum: Information Science," *Drexel Library Quarterly*, III, No. 1 (January 1967), 108-14.

Schlueter, R. A. "Information Science: Some Questions and Answers," *American Documentation*, XX, No. 4 (October 1969), 366-68.

Slamecka, V. "Graduate Programs in Information Science at the Georgia Institute of Technology," *Special Libraries*, April 1968, 246-50.

————— . "On the Methodology of Curricular Studies," *American Documentation*, XX, No. 4 (October 1969), 355-57.

Taylor, R. S. "The Interfaces Between Librarianship and Information Science and Engineering," *Special Libraries*, January 1967, 45-48.

APPENDIX
LIBRARY SCHOOL CURRICULUM

1. Introduction to Librarianship
    Basic introductory graduate level course to be taken by all new students.

2. Core Courses
    Recommended for all students, although not necessarily required.
    a. Cataloging and Classification
    b. Library Administration and Organization
    c. Reference Service and Sources
        1) Humanities ⎱ options
        2) Science ⎰

3. "Information Science"
    a. Introduction to Information Retrieval
    b. Indexing and Abstracting: Theory and Practice
    c. Vocabulary Control for Information Retrieval
    d. Evaluation of Information Products and Services
    e. The Users of Information Services: Information Flow and Information Needs

    (Note: 3a is a prerequisite for 3b-3e.)

    f. Introduction to Library Automation
    g. Advanced Automation: Systems Analysis and Programming
    h. Telecommunications in Library Applications

    (Note 3f is a prerequisite for 3g and 3h.)

    i. Scientific Management Principles Applied to Library Problems
    j. Reprography and Facsimile Transmission
    k. (Related courses from other departments, e.g., Computer Science, Linguistics)

4. Other Courses in the Curriculum
    A full range of options, including advanced courses in cataloging and classification, administration and reference work, and specialized courses of various types (e.g., children's literature, medical literature and reference work), ad infinitum (i.e., the complete spectrum of courses offered as options in an accredited school).

    (Note: There may be some justification for including 3a and 3f as "core" courses in the curriculum.)

ON CURRENT TRENDS, ISSUES AND INNOVATIONS IN PROFESSIONAL EDUCATION FOR LIBRARY AND INFORMATION SERVICE

C. Walter Stone

President
J-MARC, Inc.

Introduction

Although they are certainly becoming moot questions, this paper doesn't question either the validity or the continuing existence, for at least two decades, of separate graduate and undergraduate programs of professional education in library science. Nor does it try to make critical judgments regarding the nature and importance of separate curricula in information science, computer science or educational technology, although serious study in each of these fields is obviously very closely related to preparation for library work.

Looking beyond the turn of the present century, it seems probable that new colleges of communication science, with very broad interdisciplinary ties, will need to take on chief responsibilities for educating a majority of all educational communications media personnel including librarians. This paper closes with a plea for initiation of a national curriculum study effort based on clear formulation of learning objectives derived from searching analyses of both real and anticipated tasks which involve performance of library functions. It is hoped that this study effort will in fact be implemented with the long-range future in mind. What follows below is concerned mainly with the here and now and possibly the next 20 years.

Throughout the 1970s, one of the most difficult and important tasks of professional education for library and information service will be to recruit and prepare the new personnel needed to cope with the information explosion. This explosion, still erupting, has created a situation in which, as Jack Belzer puts it, "proliferation of published materials, the storage, retrieval, dissemination, and communication of recorded knowledge can (actually) retard our cultural progress, curtail scientific advancement, and drive us to economic disaster."[1]

In order to handle more effectively the problems created by the information explosion, libraries (and many other types of information agencies) must become increasingly ready to assimilate into their collections the mushrooming volume of information now being issued in non-print forms, as well as an ever-growing mountain of print. In order to keep pace with acquisitions, the new materials acquired must, of course, be cataloged, organized, and stored more rapidly (although for the most part still in terms of outdated conventions established originally to serve the convenience of the book and journal production industries). There must also be increasing readiness to serve the larger clienteles, expanded because of population growth, and because the importance and availability of information in new formats will become apparent to larger numbers.

Librarians and information specialists must also be prepared to comprehend and deal effectively with a much greater degree of complexity in the inter-relationships of concepts and ideas as well as the many and varied ways in which different people approach searches for knowledge.

Taking these matters into account, in recent years most colleges and universities which offer professional education for library and information service have been attempting to redefine roles, improve their faculties, modernize their teaching methods, and change or add to existing course content those educational experiences most likely to yield the sorts of new competencies desired, including—to cite just one example—ability to understand and make good use of computer services. Among changes already made or planned at a number of universities are the following:

1. A lengthening of the professional curriculum, (a) by requiring completion of two graduate years to fulfill requirements for the master's degree and develop competence in a field of specialization; and (b) by reaching down into undergraduate programs to specify additional courses and majors which must be completed before gaining admission to graduate study.

2. The injection of several new areas of study, including such complex subjects as cybernetics, computer languages, etc., into already over-crowded programs.

3. The establishment of new training programs for paraprofessional personnel.

4. Introduction of new instructional methods and technology.

5. Expansion of the number of post-degree and in-service training opportunities on a short-term basis in areas such as fiscal planning, computer use, and work with disadvantaged groups.

Responding to such proposals for change, one negative point of view voiced frequently is to the effect that professional education in library science has already become a completely indigestible stew into which almost everything may now be thrown with impunity excepting perhaps a kitchen sink. The results for too many students and even for some faculty are confusion, frustration, and disappointment and, quite naturally, a rather acute "identity" crisis. More optimistic interpretations of the situation suggest simply that current differences of opinion, however sharp, regarding the proper responsibility of library education agencies and the nature of their curricula, simply reflect a "healthy unrest" and cyclical "recurring" needs for designing and trying out new approaches.

The several sections of this paper which follow present first a brief, predictive look at the future of library and information services. Next, a number of questions are raised regarding professional curriculum relevance and adequacy. Two sections which follow comment at some length upon current programs of graduate study and the kinds of training now being offered to paraprofessional personnel. New teaching methods are appraised briefly. And finally, a general plea is made for the nationwide launching of a major curriculum redesign effort which eventually could breathe new life and significance into professional education for library and information service.

A Look to the Future

Recent "guess-timates" drawn from articles appearing in professional journals regarding the future development of library and information service programs (and related projections of manpower needs) do not preclude the possibility that most Americans may soon come to rely upon new types of local or regional communication service agencies, or "information centers," as their primary means of gaining access to the world's store of recorded knowledge. Although the "Information Center" is an entirely fictional concept, it does, however, represent the kind of organization which will be actually needed, in physical terms. The concept suggests development at the community level of something more than a typical large public library system, although less than a "people's university," combining elements of an up-to-date branch bank, a chain department store, and a social welfare counseling service.

Taking advantage of the seemingly ever-broadening range of modern electro-mechanical devices developed for information transfer and handling, local Information Centers would maintain direct access to regional, national, and even international centers. Local units would, however, be able to tap directly worldwide networking approaches to gathering, sorting, and storing of knowledge and, in light of established constituent needs, be able to initiate appropriate searches, handle information retrieval, and effect distribution (in some cases even reaching directly into a patron's home or office with a data- or picture-phone device which will soon have the additional capability of producing hard copy on demand).

Information Center personnel (including some still called librarians) will serve Center functions as representatives of various types of public and private constituencies responsible for 1) analyzing needs for knowledge, 2) making efficient use of Information Center systems and technology, and 3) providing counsel on ways and means of putting information to good use.

Expressed in overly simplified terms, the Information Center idea may be said to suggest a global service organization which, eventually, might be composed of both larger and some smaller units. Each of these units, however, would be linked to all other units in the system for purposes of achieving multi-directional communication, and all of them could be asked directly to provide service to individuals, groups, and organizations wherever located. Requests for service would be honored in terms of established levels of need and priorities based on the public consensus.

The total number of Information Center personnel needed to establish and maintain even the most basic operations (of a world knowledge service) would necessarily be large and would demand a range of expertise covering a broad spectrum of the communication sciences, arts, crafts, skills and special talents.

137

Indeed, the range of positions deemed essential may be so broad as to defy their listing at this point in time.

However, certain common knowledges would undoubtedly be required of all Information Center employees working on the professional level. Most importantly, these would include: 1) a basic understanding of human communication and learning processes; 2) familiarity with and demonstrated ability to use the apparatus, techniques, and technological systems which comprise the Information Center's ways and means of acquiring, handling, and providing access to the world's store of knowledge; 3) sufficient appreciation and awareness of one or more fields of basic human interest and endeavor to render possible the identification and sound interpretation of user needs and to utilize information center resources effectively in a patron's behalf. In short, the three prerequisite knowledges will include communication, information systems, and basic subject expertise.

The Question of Relevance

Chief among issues which divide current professional thinking about formal studies in library science are those concerning relevance. Typical questions raised by students as well as by many prospective employers reveal some deep uncertainties felt generally in the library and information service professions regarding both their present and future roles. For instance, in actuality, how much study of the current (and fairly typical) mix of the computer, library and information sciences and of mass communication and educational technology will prove relevant either to existing jobs or to positions which may develop within the next 15 to 20 years?[2] And how much attention should really be given to opportunities for specializing in school, college, community or industrial service, etc.?

At present, librarians face a difficult situation in which hard choices must be made. Taking into account predictions regarding future development of library and information service programs, and the likelihood that within just a few years "on-demand" electronic information services will reach into most American homes and offices, some major decisions must be reached soon regarding the extent to which basic library functions can and should be modified. One possible choice could well be to simply maintain and expand the traditional functions of providing base information services, making use of whatever new technologies happen to be available. An alternative could be to maintain libraries as institutions concerned only (or, at least, primarily) with print and to accept a social role of declining significance although one which is certainly appropriate and may actually be the most viable. There will always be need for the kinds of access to printed media that libraries normally have provided, even though much new material is "published" in other formats including those generated by computers. It can also be argued, with some justification, that libraries and information centers generally do not have the right combination of skills and resources to play major roles in shaping the coming use of electronic "on-demand" information services. On the other hand, the chief continuing social commitment of professional library and information serivces has always been to provide access to recorded ideas and information—a unique and vital

138

contribution to maintenance of a free society.

Among other questions raised frequently are those which ask what specific knowledges, attitudes, and skills are in fact essential to successful careers in present-day librarianship as distinguished from the knowledges, attitudes, and skills needed by information specialists? What common understandings are really important? And what differences should be acknowledged? Answers to such questions may reflect philosophical positions which are poles apart, or they may show that library and information service are perceived as belonging to the same continuum.

Basic differences may also be seen in opinions expressed concerning the separate study of information science as such. While it isn't a purpose of this paper to discuss in detail the problems of information science curriculum development, perhaps it is appropriate to note that some programs direct the primary attention of students to highly theoretical formulations concerning the nature of information and its environment. Others stress the design, development, testing, and evaluation of new information systems created to serve particular needs. And still others are mainly interested in the planning and practical management of public information services.

Professional opinions diverge even regarding the education of librarians who will serve in very traditional roles. For instance, one suggestion which has its supporters urges division of library education curricula into several broadly defined areas: 1) preparation for bibliographic and reader services; 2) social motivation and public relations services; 3) middle and higher level administration services; 4) school and children's librarianship; 5) reference and information services. Successful on-the-job performance in each of these five areas is said by advocates to require unique skills, training, and temperament, and to be cohesive within itself—thus representing a kind of sub-professional field of work which warrants separate and special study.

Another area of professional uncertainty involves study of educational technology. As one focal point of graduate professional education for library and information service, the study of educational technology represents a special interest of those preparing for media-service careers in schools, colleges, and universities. The primary aims of work in educational technology would be to develop competencies required for instructional systems design work, production of new educational materials, and to insure provision of needed counseling for optimum use of all types of learning resources.

So far so good. There does seem to be fairly wide-spread agreement on the need for competencies such as those listed, especially in schools. But the problem with educational technology is this; the field of school library media service is presently in a state of flux. Although it is moving toward several administrative mergers with allied service areas (e.g., radio-TV), in most schools the field is still made up of two major streams—one representing a special interest in audiovisual materials and equipment, and the other in books and other printed materials.[3] Typical media service programs established by even the most sophisticated school systems reflect a situation in which the school library and the AV center still exist apart from each other and are directed by separately trained professionals who report to different administrative officers.

The *Joint Standards for School Media Programs*, adopted in 1969 by the

139

American Association of School Librarians and the Department of Audiovisual (NEA) Instruction, now AECT, propose highly sophisticated media centers for both elementary and secondary schools, which will house a vast array of materials, equipment, and professional and non-professional staffs. But questions asked regarding the kinds and quality of training which should be received by those who will ultimately manage such centers are at present still unanswered. A majority of universities offer today only three relevant professional training programs: those established for training audiovisual specialists and educational technologists (generally in schools of education), and that addressed to the prospective school librarian (who, generally speaking, will take his work in a department or school of library science). What might in the future constitute optimum programs for training *all* school media specialists together or each type separately presently remain undefined, and librarians must frequently develop special multi-media competencies through participation in short courses, regional workshops, and institutes.

In short, the place of educational technology and (for that matter) of other special areas of study within professional education for library and information services remains uncertain both with respect to its relevance and in terms of its proportions. Just how much attention within a given program of study can and should be given educational technology? How important will AV knowledges and skills gained through given studies actually prove to be in the future? At present, the educational information and communication service professions do not agree on answers to these questions.

Toward New Professional Curricula

In order to get and keep a job as a librarian one usually has to "join the union"—i.e., complete a one- or two-year master's degree program of study which has been accredited by the American Library Association (that does not include school librarians). State requirements differ but, generally speaking, school librarians, who must start with a valid teaching credential, may be employed after completion of something less than a full year of library science, provided certain courses have been taken. Typically, courses specified by state education authorities are those which assist development of basic skills such as those needed for simple cataloging. Admission to graduate programs of professional education accredited by ALA normally assumes the prior completion of work for one or more bachelor's degrees with or without formal course work in library science or related fields. Encouraged in the published catalogs of most library schools, although not very often demanded, is a significant degree of background study either in the humanities or in the physical and social sciences.

A typical fifth-year master's program in library school begins by providing remedial education when necessary—usually in a sequence of four or more "core" courses designed to introduce basic library functions and the nature of professional responsibilities for selecting materials, reference service, cataloging and classification. (Prerequisite for those planning to major in information science or to specialize in that field alone is advanced work in mathematics and some knowledge of computer programming.) The balance of work completed for

140

a master's degree normally includes one or more courses which deal with library technical services, reference functions, materials, mechanized approaches to information storage and retrieval, general principles of administration, and management of a particular kind of library or information center. For school librarians, a significant period of field work is also required. Elective areas of study may include consideration of library development abroad, library education, or provision of service to special groups.

The chief goal of most post-master's work, other than that which provides opportunities for true specialization—for instance, in information science—or which leads into study for a doctorate, involves acquisition of special skills and/or the "retreading" of individuals who may have been working in the field for some years and who need urgently to have their store of professional knowledge and skills brought up to date. Completion of work for a Ph.D. is usually reserved for those interested in teaching and research careers or in managing larger libraries.

In most cases, the typical fifth-year master's program is a sort of a "once over lightly" kind of activity intended to yield at the end of 12 months or so a new crop of "professionals." By definition, "professional tasks" (in librarianship) are those which require a special background and education on the basis of which library needs can be identified, problems analyzed, goals set, and original and creative solutions formulated. Such tasks usually involve abilities to integrate theory into practice and provide necessary leadership in planning, organizing, communicating, and administering programs of service to those who make use of library materials and services. In planning library service for "users," the *professional* person recognizes potential users as well as current ones, and designs services which will reach all who can benefit from them.[4]

It's a "tall order." And the simple truth is that this vague description, typical of the rationale which still underlies a good many programs of graduate study in accredited library schools, is really satisfying to no one—not to the students, to the faculty, or to prospective employers. Real understanding and appreciation of information science, for example, would require a full year's separate and special study in itself. The same is true of educational technology. To become properly qualified for positions in either of these two fields may well involve completion of a second, third, and even a fourth year of advanced graduate work, often of an inter-disciplinary nature touching fields as widely separated as philosophy and industrial engineering.

In recognition of the superficiality of too many fifth- and even some sixth-year master's programs, with their heavy emphasis on familiarization with processes, techniques, and technology, there has been a tendency in recent years to suggest that any knowledges and skills common to library and information service professions should be acquired in undergraduate preparation. One promising effort in this direction is represented in a recent definition of master's program responsibility developed by a curriculum study group at the University of Pittsburgh's Graduate School of Library and Information Science.[5] This definition rejects flatly the idea that a four-year liberal arts education, or four-year preparation for teaching in school, can be expected to yield readiness for graduate study. Since even the area of "liberal arts" cannot itself be defined readily, the Pittsburgh faculty study group abandoned the attempt and actually specified completion of a new model undergraduate program. Only after completion of this program could master's work be authorized. Students enrolling in the undergraduate program would be expected to obtain a strong foundation in the methodologies of three major branches of knowledge—humanities, behavioral science and natural science—and would be introduced to those points of view most likely to yield a real sense of belonging to the "family of men" (e.g., a concept sometimes gained through studies of cultures and civilizations). Knowledge of how to function effectively in today's world is to be helped by studies of probability and statistics. Completion of a second major exclusive of library science would be required so that each student could develop depth in one or more of the main methodologies.

An implicit assumption which underlies proposals for new undergraduate curricula is that most non-library oriented courses would in fact overlap with courses in library science in such ways that each could reinforce the others. For instance, the general college course in civilizations can and probably should include significant material on social roles of mass communications and the importance of information records in the development of societies—a thought which suggests, incidentally, that most existing texts for such courses might not prove adequate.

Also implied in specification of a new undergraduate curriculum leading to advanced work in library or information science is the view that it no longer makes sense to rely on a simple "stacking" of more or less isolated courses which in the past have so often represented the typical undergraduate preparation of students enrolling in library school. Needed today is a frankly tougher and more realistic approach.

The Pittsburgh proposals do not say that graduates of the prescribed undergraduate program will have become skilled "practitioners" in any area of library or information service. They would, however, be expected to have become at least "promising apprentices." And so the primary goal of the master's program which follows would then (assuming deficiencies have been made up) be one of insuring satisfactory completion of foundation work in research methodologies of the natural sciences, mathematics, esthetics and behavioral sciences as a kind of "new" core curriculum. The balance of work to be introduced would stress analysis, design, evaluation, and control of libraries and library operations.

Opportunity to specialize in a field of interest would be accommodated by providing for separate study of various types of library operations including management, technical processes, information service, collections development and maintenance, and the design and use of management information systems. Required for receipt of the master's degree would be demonstrable mastery of fundamental research methods and tool subjects including the following: ability to design experiments, classification, automation and communications theory, management information system principles, and operations research. For those who wish to proceed beyond the master's degree, the Pittsburgh study rounds out the picture by recommending a Ph.D. program for development of "scholars who can create principles, laws and theories, evaluate them and interpret them in the profession."[6]

Although admittedly unique to the institution, the University of Pittsburgh's proposals for modification and improvement of the professional curricula in library science may very well reflect a national trend in serious thinking about the field; i.e., new programs will be increasingly inter-disciplinary; they should begin in undergraduate years and cover a broader range of subject matter as well as professional work areas; they should be able to guarantee more in the way of immediate competency to perform successfully on a job following completion of first degree work; and, while allowing for some specialization, they should continue to encourage development of generalists who can adapt to many kinds of working environments.

In the author's view, perhaps the most important aspect of the Pittsburgh curriculum proposals (and of similar recommendations advanced by other like-minded library school faculties) is represented in the idea that to serve the future well, professional studies should begin immediately following graduation from secondary school. Such proposals reveal the incredible naiveté of library schools that expect a one- or two-year graduate program to yield (as from the head of Zeus) responsible library managers. Yet perhaps equally or more naive is that point of view which holds that "librarianship" is a single profession. More fruitful, in the author's opinion, would be a frank acknowledgment that library and information service agencies now require an expanding cluster of many types of clerical, technical, operational, and administrative personnel. No single program of professional education can be judged valid for all who choose to enter the field. Common elements which do exist should be identified and cultivated during undergraduate years. In the future, many new types of graduate programs should be devised keyed to task analyses which clearly identify manpower requirements. And when considering such requirements, special effort should be taken to avoid placing undue emphasis on operational techniques and technology (which undergo virtually constant change) as distinguished from fostering understandings of both the variety and depth of the human needs for information and ways in which these are best satisfied. The need is *not* to produce more masters of diverse technical minutiae.

On Training Paraprofessionals[7]

Having suggested the de-emphasis of techniques and technology in graduate professional study for library service, perhaps it should be pointed out that these subjects are, however, of prime importance in training paraprofessional personnel. Most deans, directors, program chairmen, and others having responsibility for design of new curricula suitable for the training of paraprofessional personnel (aides, technicians, associates, *et al.*) would agree. Especially troublesome, however, are nagging questions of instructional level, duration of studies, proper sequencing, and teaching methods—not to mention admission requirements.

First, with respect to levels of study, what roles can be played by paraprofessionals in libraries and information agencies? How should library technicians be trained? What kinds of existing work in libraries and information service agencies actually require completion of two years of college, or of four years, and where should professional education begin and end?

"Off-the-cuff" answers to these questions suggest that increasing numbers of prarprofessional staff members will soon be needed to provide clerical or technical assistance in libraries and that, sometimes, performance of such unique tasks as might be represented in managing a community "outreach" program could lead to employment of paraprofessionals who might be "a little short" of professional training, but whose personal traits or unique background of life experience would make them effective on the job.

In most cases, however, the chief role to be served by aides and technicians is to free "career" staff (so-called) to engage in more professional work, by which is usually meant performance of tasks involving independent judgment, interpretation of rules and procedures, formulation of original and creative solutions to problems, etc.

The typical library roster of paraprofessional employees includes: aides (whose primary training will be gained on the job); technicians or technical assistants, often trained in library technology programs developed for undergraduates in either lower- or upper-division classes; and those in the category of library associate. As set forth in a policy statement adopted by the Council of the American Library Association on June 30, 1970, the category of associate

> assumes a need for an educational background like that represented by a bachelor's degree from a good four-year institution of higher learning in the United States. Assignments given to an associate may be such that library knowledge is less important than general education. And whether the title is Library Associate or Associate Specialist depends on the nature of the tasks and specific responsibilities assigned. Persons holding a B.A. degree, with or without the library science minor or practical experience in libraries, are eligible for appointment in this category.... The Associate category also provides opportunity for persons of promise and exceptional talent to begin library employment below the level of professionals . . . thus to combine regular work in the library with course work at the graduate level. Where this kind of work/study arrangement is made, a combination of work and formal study should provide (1) increasing responsibility within the Associate ranks as the individual moves through the academic program, and (2) eligibility for promotion upon completion of the master's degree to positions of professional responsibility and attendant reclassification to the professional category.

In the past, professional librarians have notoriously been overburdened with a seemingly never-ending and always-expanding number of clerical tasks and technical routines. As a result, development of the paraprofessional career idea and of related training programs has seemed most welcome. In actual practice, however, paraprofessional personnel (especially those employed on technician levels) have often encountered strong resistance to their positions and frequently have been assigned undemanding work to limit their chances for advancement.

Problems to be faced by those planning the education of paraprofessional personnel include the lack of clear job descriptions that could suggest the types of training most needed. Also, recent economic conditions have made some professional people more willing to work on technician levels, and the problem is compounded when smaller libraries, unable to support a variety of individuals

144

with special skills, instead employ a multi-purpose staff. Added to these are the unresolved problems of certification and credentialling. The result is that effective planning, design and development of sound competency-based programs of paraprofessional instruction become very difficult. One unkind appraisal sometimes given is that too many of the library technology programs developed so far represent "watered down" and out-of-date versions of old-fashioned professional education.

Another argument sometimes advanced against extensive development of paraprofessional education programs for library and information service is that the lower pay scales that aides, technicians and associates command can easily undermine professional salary schedules. That is, general administrative acceptance of the need for hiring "professional" as distinguished from paraprofessional personnel may well decline because, in the opinion of some employers, the primary work which needs doing can be accomplished better and cheaper by non-professionals.

In marked opposition to negative views of library technician training programs are those which strongly support its development. One such view results from the present state of flux in the school library media field mentioned previously. Recent changes in educational curricula and in the methods of formal instruction have established a need for a considerable increase in the number of school media specialists who should be recruited and trained even within the present decade. Jobs to be assigned media aides, technicians and other specialists employed in schools and also on the college campus will grow out of new service program responsibilities. These include responsibility for production (and necessary reproduction) of instructional materials; operations and maintenance of new kinds of equipment; development of new technical routines required to support, for instance, computer-assisted, -managed or -controlled instruction; and eventual *automation* of library circulation, reference, and processing functions. Although labeled by some a contentious issue, few educational leaders still doubt the available statistics, which show that the number of paraprofessionals needed for school library centers can easily exceed the number that can be recruited and properly trained.

One additional point should probably be made before moving on. This point concerns the location of paraprofessional training programs and the typical non-transferability of academic credits received. A good many library technician training programs are being set up in junior or community colleges as two-year terminal curricula. To this point, little has been done to insure the possibility of orderly transition from such programs into the mainstream of professional education. Without wishing to press the matter too hard, certainly it would seem desirable for future library technicians as well as professional personnel to receive their preparation for work in the field in parallel programs which are carefully coordinated so each knows something about the responsibilities of the other, so that the duplication of training activities can be avoided, and so that the career ladder (or lattice) concept now being recommended generally within the profession can be advanced by creating more "bridges" from one program to another. Unfortunately, at the present time some students as well as faculty in accredited library graduate schools think of paraprofessional training as something "lower" and/or "way out there."

Concerning Instructional Methods and Media

In addition to the professional and paraprofessional curriculum content and organization, the special attention of library and information science educators should also be focused on the methods and means of instruction employed. Contrary to opinions sometimes expressed by students and practitioners about "antiquated methods of teaching commonly used in library schools," it can fairly be said that failure to use present-day techniques and technology isn't really a basic problem.

The "square box" classrooms, cataloging laboratories, "monk's cell" offices, and incomplete libraries still exist in a few institutions. But this picture is changing rapidly. Audiovisual media (that is, films, filmstrips, slides, graphics, cassettes and kits, which may include combinations of these to be used together with printed resources) now constitute a significant portion of the instructional resources inventory maintained by most professional schools (even if they are sometimes housed in poorly designed, out-of-reach cabinets). Regular use of closed-circuit television to assist instruction no longer represents an "extraordinary effort" in library and information science courses. And "on-line" access to computer service via local terminals placed in library school offices or laboratories is no longer thought "unusual."

Ten years ago, perhaps even five years ago, such statements couldn't have been taken seriously. But today, although their slowness in arriving did block recognition of real and very dramatic changes which have taken place in the development of improved teaching methods, materials, and facilities, it can be acknowledged honestly that a revolution (however quiet) has been experienced in little more than a decade, and results of this revolution can now be seen in library schools across the country.

Also developed in recent years is widespread interest in work-study programs established in partnership with cooperating schools, colleges, and many public and special libraries. If the use of video tape recordings for training individuals in reference procedures, story-telling, and reader's advisory work isn't yet widespread, it is not uncommon. Computer facilities of one sort or another can be found in most major library schools. And the use of cassette tapes, filmstrips, and slides for self-instruction in many subjects has already become an established technique.

Field trips to libraries, museums, and information agencies serving the region in which a given school is located represent a significant aspect of professional training offered today. In addition, there is increasing emphasis given to wholly independent study, use of faculty mainly as tutors, and development of new approaches to course work (for example, in research methods, where direct participation with faculty in actual surveys or field research projects is, in some schools, the primary method of instruction used).

Taking into account needs for specialization, in recent years a number of professional schools have developed programs which feature preparation for multi-media services. For instance, California State University in San Jose and Southern Illinois University have achieved some distinction in this field. Computer work is believed to be an especially strong feature of programs offered at the University of Pittsburgh, Rutgers, Syracuse and the University of

California in both Berkeley and Los Angeles. Undergraduate and mixed level programs which have special promise in terms of employing new methods of instruction can be found at Arizona State University and at the University of Colorado, among others.

In short, professional education for librarianship and information services, insofar as instructional methods and media are concerned, is in 1973 a different experience from that once considered typical. At first, some faculty have resisted "inroads" made by those media believed to encroach upon their information-presenting duties or responsibilities. But, once they have used new media comfortably, such resistance normally disappears.

There is, however, one very fundamental problem which hasn't yet received sufficient professional attention. That problem relates to instructional goals and objectives. Except for a few research and management seminars that increasingly feature case study approaches (and to that extent enable students to comprehend more readily what librarianship and information service mean in actual practice), professional education and library information science is still conducted by and large without enabling the students to gain any very reliable sense of competencies needed. They do not know exactly how much can and should be learned in how much time or how best to pursue or follow up professional learning activities on one's own. Typical courses in library science, even at places where extensive (and often costly) syllabi have been compiled, too often constitute more or less random and sterile exposures to the names of places, people, and events considered more or less representative of a given professional area, while the student is left to his own devices to figure out which attitudes, specific skills, and knowledges must be acquired to do useful work. Fortunately, there is now a growing interest in trying to do a better job of orienting students to the desired work outcomes. But, with exceptions, library and information science programs remain fairly vague about learning objectives, and the majority of courses in library science haven't yet been subjected to expert analysis for the derivation of teaching objectives which then can be stated in behavioral terms. Nor have standards of competency been determined. As a consequence, a true sense of relevance to actual on-the-job performance all too often is lacking. And this comment brings the train of thought back, in a more or less circular fashion, to a point which was made at the start of this paper.

Needed: A National Curriculum Study

That single task which is now most vital to the improvement of professional education for library and information service in the future involves the identification of goals and formulation of clearly stated learning objectives in terms of which improved instructional methods and media can be devised and put to good use and what valid measures of performance can be defined and applied to these objectives. To date, this task has been undertaken only in a very few places and mostly on a sporadic basis. Usually, the need for this effort, if recognized, remains ignored and where not ignored simply doesn't provoke any action.

Purely local criticisms of professional curricula in library science will not be helpful. The difficulties of producing sound professional curricula based on

147

clearly defined objectives and stated in behavioral terms, and of developing appropriate new teaching methodologies, are enormous and shouldn't be left for each institution to resolve for itself. What must be encouraged, therefore, is the launching of a library (and information) science curriculum design effort which will begin with the detailed specification of competencies needed to perform satisfactorily in both present and prospective library and information service positions; these competencies will be determined in the light of hard data gained from manpower studies and rigorous task analyses. Necessarily, such an effort must take on the proportions of a major project of the library and information service professions. In its own way, it could resemble work done several years ago in creating for secondary education "new physics," "new math," "new chemistry," and the fruits of BSCS (the Biological Sciences Curriculum Study).

If attention of this sort can be given to the job, and if the dollar resources needed to implement the required changes are provided (which would probably require federal subsidy), future professional education for library and information services could well become more truly relevant and cost effective. It would also be more personally satisfying preparation for employment in what is now acknowledged in many quarters to be the world's most important occupation—provision of knowledge availability.

FOOTNOTES

[1] Jack Belzer, "The Conference Theme," *American Documentation*, XX (October 1969), 329

[2] Difficulties likely to be encountered in reconciling differences among related fields can be seen readily from even the most cursory examination of existing curricular plans as shown in the Appendix to this paper.

[3] *A Manpower Survey of the School Library Media Field*, report submitted to U.S. Office of Education by Social, Educational Research and Development, Inc. (Silver Spring, Md., August 15, 1972).

[4] Council of the American Library Association, *Library Education and Manpower*, June 30, 1970, p. 3.

[5] *Education for Librarianship*, Graduate School of Library Science, University of Pittsburgh, January 1972. (Mimeographed.)

[6] *Ibid.*, p. 14.

[7] This section draws importantly from Dorothy F. Deininger's excellent summary, *Paraprofessionals in Libraries and Media Centers* (paper prepared for U.S. Office of Education, n.d.).

BIBLIOGRAPHY

Belzer, Jack. "The Conference Theme." *American Documentation*, XX (October 1969), 329.

——————— , ed. "Information Science Education: Curriculum Development and Evaluation (Proceedings, Curriculum Committees of Special Interest Group on Education in Information Science)." *American Documentation*, XX (October 1969), 327-76.

Boll, John J. "The Basis for Library Education." *Library Quarterly*, XLII (April 1972), 195-210.

Carnegie Commission on Higher Education. *The Fourth Revolution, Instructional Technology in Higher Education*. New York: McGraw-Hill, 1972.

Council of the American Library Association. *Library Education and Manpower*. Chicago: American Library Association, June 30, 1970.

Deininger, Dorothy J. *Paraprofessionals in Libraries and Media Centers*. Undated paper prepared for U.S. Office of Education, Rutgers University.

Education for Librarianship, A Preliminary Report of the Professional Education Task Group at the Graduate School of Library and Information Sciences. Pittsburgh, Pa.: GSLIS, Univ. of Pittsburgh, January 1972.

Ely, Donald P., ed. *The Field of Educational Technology: A Statement of Definition*. Paper developed for the Association of Educational Communication and Technology, n.d.

Library Education Division, American Library Association. "Criteria for Programs to Prepare Library/Media Technical Assistants." *American Libraries*, II, No. 10 (Nov. 1971), 1059-63.

A Manpower Survey of the School Library Media Field. Report submitted to U.S. Office of Education by Social, Educational Research and Development, Inc. Silver Spring, Md., August 15, 1972.

Mignon, Edmond, ed. *Directions in Education for Information Science*. Proceedings of a Symposium, Denver, Colorado, November 11-13, 1971. Washington, D.C.: American Society for Information Sciences.

Parker, Edwin B. "Libraries and Information Utility." Paper invited by the Information Science and Automation Division of the American Library Association. Chicago: ALA, June 28, 1972.

Taylor, Robert S. "Toward an Educational Base for the Information Sciences and Information Engineering." *Education for Information Science*. Washington, D.C.: Spartan Books, 1965, pp. 77-81.

APPENDIX
A SAMPLE DISPLAY OF EDUCATION INFORMATION AND COMMUNICATION SERVICE CURRICULA

(Master's Level)

	a. Educational Technology	b. Library Science	c. School Library/Media
Prerequisites:	Intro. to Ed. Media	Selection of materials Basic Reference materials	Foundations Collections Processing Management
	* * * * * *	* * * * * *	* * * * * *
Required:	Production of Instr. Resources Development of IMC Concept Administration of Ed. Media Library Techniques for Instr. Materials	Technical Services Foundations of Librarianship School Media Serv. Public Library Serv. College Lib. Serv. Special Lib. Serv.	Curriculum Ed. Psychology Quality Verification
	* * * * * *	* * * * * *	* * * * * *
Choose From:	Introduction to Instruc. TV Advanced ITV Workshop Characteristics of Computer based instruction and curriculum Principles of Automated Teaching & Programmed Learning Seminars & Practicums in Programmed Learning Field Experience in Ed. Media Educational Film Production Photographic Techniques in Education	Literature for Children Literature of Soc. (or) Sciences (or) Literature of Humanities (or) Literature of Science Thesis (or) Research Materials	Photography & Graphics Technology & Instr. SLM Issues and Problems Internship or Practicum
	* * * * * *	* * * * * *	* * * * * *
	(electives)	(electives)	(electives)

	d. Information Science (Summary)		e. Computer Science (Summary)
	Intro. to Info. theory	Prerequisites:	Calculus Programming
Level I— Undergrad.	Intro. to Programming Numerical Analysis Gy Arithmic Langs. Statistical Computations Intro. to Linguistics Data Processing		

* * * * * *

Level II— Grad.	Programming Language Design Simulation Techniques Info. Stor. & Retrieval Computer Design & Organization Processing of Natural & Artificial Languages Statistical Computations Systems Analysis Computer Systems	Required:	Symbolic Logic Recursive Functions Information Theory Computer Hardware Compiler Construction Data Base Management Information Retrieval Systems

* * * * * *

Level III— Advanced Grad.	Computationed Statistics Man-machine Communication Automation and Switching Theory Graphics Theory Theoretical Foundations of Info. Science		

* * * * * *

	(electives)		(electives)

a. Temple University
b. Cal-State University, San Jose
c. Arizona State University
d.&e. Courses said to be offered in most departments
(See *American Documentation*, Oct. 1969, pp. 360, 361, & 365)

151

PLANNING FOR CHANGE IN LIBRARY EDUCATION:
SUMMARY AND RECOMMENDATIONS FOR ACTION

Martha Boaz

Dean
School of Library Science
University of Southern California

It is agreed that change is needed in library education; there is no agreement, however on the nature of the change. The material which follows is summarized in part from several papers which were commissioned on the general subject; other statements are derived from the discussion and recommendations which came out of the two-day conference held to discuss the papers; and still other ideas and suggestions are those of the author of this chapter. These fall roughly into the following categories: 1) the general philosophical concept of the role of the library in society and of the responsibility or library education within this total concept; 2) library education curricula; 3) various library education tracks; 4) the need for leadership in the field.

The Role of the Library in Society

The library plays an important and responsible role in society. This role will become increasingly important as the need for information becomes critical in a more complex society. The traditional passive role of the library should be replaced by active involvement in the dissemination of information. In the past we have waited for people to come to the library; in the future we must take the library to the people. The library must reexamine its role and its responsibility for the dissemination of information that influences the world. The library profession must be aware and ready for the many changes in society that are inevitable in the course of human events. And these changes are likely to be of an incredible magnitude. One of the directors of the Stanford Research Institute predicts that the change in the next 30 years may equal the change of the past two or three centuries. It is highly likely that the library will become a center for activities not traditionally associated with it and that information centers will become influential change agents. There will be more library involvement with other community, business, and government agencies.

In order to cope with the problems and progress of future years, the library must be informed and able both to adapt to change and to initiate change in libraries and in library education. After determining their reason for being and establishing their objectives, libraries and information centers must study the needs of their users and must design programs for fulfilling these needs. At the same time the library education curricula should prepare information specialists to give the client the services he needs.

The library education of the future should be planned to accommodate new social and organizational forms. The needs of the times will determine the values which people want, and these values will determine goals. It seems highly likely that libraries of the future may become community information centers; that libraries will be only one form of many information service organizations; and that the publications will become much more diverse in form and format than they are today. In order to get ready for these and other changes, plans should be prepared now, for the future is too important to be left to chance. Professional planners point out that plans should be developed for alternate futures, since otherwise events may proceed to a point where only one choice is possible and no decision allowed.

Library Education Curricula

Three items are generally involved in curriculum construction: 1) curriculum content, 2) curriculum length, and 3) curriculum organization.

One of the first steps in planning curriculum is to set up the objectives and goals of the professional program. Next, there should be a list of the behavioral objectives, the specific competencies and professional skills every graduate should have in order to perform the services which will be required of him when he is a member of the profession. After these have been decided, a variety of experiences should be arranged that will be appropriate to develop the objectives of the curriculum and to contribute to the development of a professional librarian and information specialist. The plans should include different levels and types of education, from the paraprofessional to the research scholar; the plans should also provide for individual personal specialization within the curriculum and, as specific needs are further outlined, should prepare persons to meet the particular requirements of different types of libraries and information centers. Then a set of alternate curricula should be outlined.

It has been suggested that the systems approach be used in designing a library school curriculum. Martha Jane Zachert proposed for the special library an approach which seems appropriate for other libraries. This approach includes the following steps: 1) establish the objectives of the curriculum; 2) identify the components of the library/information system; 3) define the human jobs; 4) specify the acceptable performance of each component of the human job; 5) reexamine the performance within the total environment; 6) consider the resources and restraints; 7) postulate the curriculum; 8) test the plan; and 9) redesign.

The General Curriculum

Granted that the educational program should be based on the general competencies required to give the services the public wants, the curriculum would focus on: 1) the purpose and function of libraries and information sources; 2) building collections, organizing them for uses, retrieving and interpreting informational sources; 3) applying basic functions to type of clientele; and 4) applying tool skills such as systems analysis, statistical methods, cost accounting, computer programming, and general communications techniques.

Interdisciplinary Study

Interdisciplinary study is highly recommended in a program that spreads over a considerable time span. Certain constraints, however, hamper interdisciplinary study in a one-year graduate professional program. Desirable and interesting as courses in other schools are, it seems unwise to include many of them. This is the only year many students will ever have for pursuing the library school courses that will give them the most specific and immediate preparation for their professional careers. Indeed, there are many additional courses in the library school which would be highly desirable for the student but which he cannot take because of the short time span. There have been frequent suggestions that library school students take courses in administration and management in the school of business. If this recommendation is followed, one hopes that the library school students may be put into special groups and that the teachers in charge will give particular attention to library problems. Within the interdisciplinary framework, from another direction, the library school might offer courses for other departments of the university. Appropriate courses could survey the bibliographical and information resources of a particular discipline and demonstrate how these resources could be used most effectively.

Library schools may expand or merge with other departments to form communications and information science colleges with a common core program and several special purpose programs in areas such as information systems, instructional technology, and information science.

Information Science

Within the curriculum information science has received considerable attention in late years, and there is a fairly general consensus that all library school students should be required to have at least a minimum level of knowledge in this field. Graduates working in an automated environment will have to be able to adapt to and make use of knowledge-transfer machinery as it applies to library operations and services. The same theory applies to non-print and audiovisual materials and to the whole area of instructional technology. Graduates should be familiar with and able to design and use the techniques and technological systems of library and information centers.

The Library in the Community

Instruction about the library in the political process should be incorporated into the curriculum. Within this framework, extensive use of publicity and public relations techniques should be stressed, for through these devices the library will be able to pursue and implement its objectives and gain support for its continuation. Librarians will learn how to become more proficient in working with public officials and government agencies.

Attention in the curriculum should also be given to developing skills in "market analysis" for library services and to the "packaging" of ideas for better ways to reach various constituent groups in the population; there should be information about how to administer library consortia and networks and how to make use of the most modern communications technology. More stress will be laid on working with lay advisors and advisory boards in order to keep the professional schools in touch with the practical world.

Research

Increasing emphasis is being placed on the value of research in libraries and on stronger research orientation, course work, and practice in research for the library school student. It has been suggested that the library profession should have a National Institute of Research and that each library school should have a research component within the school. Emphasis on research by each school and a budget allocation for a research institute within every curriculum would probably advance the library profession more rapidly than any other single effort.

Practice Work

"Practice work" or internship, abandoned in the early 1950s, is coming back into style again and is popular with students. It provides a "hands-on" live experience and a practical relationship to current practice. Several alternative types of practice work are possible: that which is very brief and part of a regular class assignment; that which is a semester or longer in duration, which is formally scheduled and supervised, and which receives course credit; that in which two people hold one job and attend school during alternate terms; and that which is similar to the traditional internship pattern with the student doing one year of supervised practice work after course work has been completed, then writing a report for the library school. The practice work is relatively easy to include in a two-year program, but it presents problems if it is a substantial internship in a one-year curriculum. It is difficult to crowd this into an already-full course load. Definitive answers have not been found about "practice work," but it seems reasonable to assume that there will be more dependence upon cooperative arrangements for work-study programs and more association with practitioners in the field.

Specialization

Specialization in professional practice allows persons with special abilities or interests to work in those areas of greatest appeal to them. From another point of view, it may be necessary to plan for more specialization for future librarians as government agencies take over a larger role in providing social services. In addition to subject specialists and bibliographers, it is likely that more persons holding doctoral degrees will be needed for positions requiring specialized, intellectual, and scholarly backgrounds. It is proposed that the library schools train specialists and prepare them for certification, and that this preparation should include substantial study and probably be followed with an examination, as is the custom in medicine.

Teaching Devices and the Quality of Teaching

The quality of teaching should improve and more innovative methods for delivering educational services should be developed. New technology and programmed materials will be available to improve and supplement teaching. Video tapes, cassettes, films, filmstrips and multiple other instructional aids are available now. It has been suggested that closed circuit television courses could be "beamed" to the library and taken by small library classes of library staff members, thus saving time and travel expense to the university. The University of Southern California Library School offered one brief introductory course of 36 half-hour programs on a regular television channel two years ago, but the regular courses have not been offered on television to this date. The idea of independent study should also be explored, for the library is a strong potential for the promotion of self instruction and for independent study.

In the near future the approach to learning will probably change from the typical formal course structure to a highly flexible atmosphere with extensive use of independent study, programmed instructional materials, simulation exercises and other methods.

It is predicted that internationally owned satellites will be used soon for mass communications. Certainly professional schools should be in the vanguard in investigating possibilities for working with this type of development.

Retraining and Continuing Education

Retraining will be required as technology changes. More vocational programs will be required, also, and there will be more need for continuing education as automation and specializations change. Extension courses should be offered at convenient geographical locations. Continuing education courses will assist the professional person to 1) attain specialized knowledge; 2) update his knowledge and keep abreast of new developments in his field; 3) improve his work performance; 4) work towards promotion; and 5) find self-fulfillment.

The Master's Degree in Library Science should be considered as only the beginning, not the end of professional study. As one librarian has said, the professional role is not static; instead it should be dynamic and should require "constant attention and continuing endeavor to take the minimally accepted level of competence at the beginning of a career and build on it to create a level of competence at any time thereafter which persons in the field would deem suitable for a person with similar experience."

The concept of continuing education has been well accepted in theory, but it has not been widely implemented in practice. However, there will be stronger incentives if credentialing and state licensing are adopted and if people are required to renew and update their credentials. An added impetus would be a system of promotions and salary increases for persons who improve their performance by continuing their education.

Credentialing Agencies

It is likely that institutions other than schools will serve as credentialing agencies in the future. If the present system of examinations and grading is discontinued, such agencies will be needed to certify that a graduate has certain competencies. The procedures might well be similar to those of the legal profession with its state bar examinations.

The proponents of state certification for librarians and for reciprocity in certification feel that the profession would be greatly strengthened by such measures. The image of the librarian would improve and gain in stature and in respect if state certification were in force.

Inter-Campus Cooperation with Other Library Schools

Related to curriculum are certain allied, procedural, and organizational matters. These involve more exchange of credits from one school to another and allowing students to take courses on two or more campuses within the same semester. There could be a planned interchange of faculties and more cooperation, in general, among library schools. It seems feasible and desirable that students have more options in planning their course of study and more opportunities for choice of courses and alternate curricula from one campus to another.

Several Library Education Tracks

It has been suggested that several parallel library education programs be offered in one institution, that these be planned and coordinated to avoid duplication and to advance the career ladder concept. The various tracks within a school could include: 1) a paraprofessional program; 2) the regular professional Master's Degree program; 3) the Doctor of Library Science program; 4) the Doctor of Philosophy program; and 5) a continuing education program. These tracks, included in one total plan, could provide direction and quality in each track according to its objectives, and at the same time ensure a lack of duplication in coverage from one track to the next one. It has been predicted that degree requirements for librarians may change to include two or more years of undergraduate study as well as two years at the master's level.

The library profession might gain in strength of professional content and in status and in prestige if professional studies could begin in the undergraduate program. There might then be a de-emphasis on techniques and technology in the graduate program. The training of paraprofessionals could also point to a better image for the graduate professional librarian, for use of paraprofessionals frees the professional librarian to do more professional work.

Special education courses, workshops, seminars, and institutes offered by appropriate agencies would be of value for volunteer workers as well as for non-credentialed staff and technicians. In addition to the short term or even a semester-long continuing education programs there must be more extensive and in-depth educational opportunities.

Library education curricula should offer sufficient tracks and levels to enable people to move from one level of professional competence to another and to recognize that there are different levels of competence. These competencies should change as higher levels of skill and expertise are required.

Leadership Needed

The most important factors to consider in building a strong library school are the caliber of the faculty and the quality of the student body. A sufficient number of distinguished people in these two categories can make a great school. Interrelated in the total picture is the need for leadership. This is probably the single greatest need in the library profession today. Leaders are needed in libraries and especially in library education, for the library school should be leading the profession. The identification and attraction into the field of a small coterie of potential young leaders with brilliant minds, leadership ability and dedication to librarianship could do more to advance the profession than a hundred plans on paper which are never implemented.

Recommendations for Action

First Steps

In order to implement the many theories which have been given in conferences and in papers concerned with change in library education, the following steps and procedures are suggested:

1. Report suggestions given at this conference to the Association of American Library Schools, the Library Education Division of the American Library Association, the National Commission on Libraries and Information Science, and to Ralph Conant, who has received a grant to study library education.

2. Seek a coordinator who is interested in the design of modern curricula for library schools.

3. Form a group of library school deans who are willing to experiment with curriculum reform within their schools.

4. Ask each dean to appoint a young faculty member to work on the project.

5. Study what other professions are doing and, if appropriate, adopt or adapt whatever principles and guidelines may be applicable to library education.

6. Use papers from this conference as a base from which to advance the curriculum design from general objectives to specific goals.

    a. Have working papers drafted covering specific areas of study.

    b. Set up a meeting to review the material produced and refine it.

    c. Distribute the refined model as an aid to curriculum revision at individual schools.

    d. Hold workshops for teachers in selected curriculum areas.

7. Take an inventory and disseminate promising practices used in library education programs.

8. Seek funding for the development, evaluation, and dissemination of model programs.

9. Establish prototype experimental model programs in at least six schools.

    a. Begin with one or two sections of a curriculum (a small-scale experiment), if it is not feasible to change the whole program.

    b. Plan alternates within the prototype(s).

10. Develop plans for several tracks, within one school, ranging from paraprofessional, Master's Degree, professional doctorate, Ph.D. Degree and on to continuing education at all levels.

    a. Articulate the various levels and design equivalency tests, such as those of CLEP, to be used as a basis for transfer credit.

11. Plan for a national curriculum study that would propose common standards, stimulate more unity in the professional preparation in library and information science programs and propose greater cooperation among all professional groups concerned with improving the quality of library education.

Long Range Plans

Although the suggestions listed below may be of interest for implementation within the near future, it is likely that logistics cannot be developed for early action. For this reason the term "long range" is used.

It is recommended:

1. That inter-university and inter-library school agreements between different institutions be encouraged to provde for the following: a) students of one library school taking a specified course or courses at another library school; b) the transferability of credit thus obtained, c) the exchange of teachers between and among library schools.

2. That professional library and educational associations work with and advise library schools in planning and providing progressive and innovative developments within their degree programs and in their continuing education and special programs.

3. That information be obtained about and use studies made of what other professions are doing in their educational programs and, when feasible, use ideas gleaned from these studies.

4. That an advisory council for library education be established in each state, the members to be appointed by the chancellor of the university system in cooperation with the state superintendent of education; that private colleges and universities be invited to participate and have a representative on the council (under same policy as that of the state university).

5. That a national certification program be set up and that certification be required of all librarians who expect to qualify as professionals. Classification and qualification standards should be devised for various levels from the beginning professional to those with supervisory and administrative responsibilities.

If these recommendations are followed, will the library school curricula of the future be very different from those of today? Will they be similar or very much the same as those of today? Nobody knows. The future cannot be predicted with certainty, but an attempt at crystal ball reading should be helpful and it will surely be interesting.

BIOGRAPHICAL SKETCHES
OF THE AUTHORS

MARTHA BOAZ

Martha Boaz has been Dean of the School of Library Science, University of Southern California, since 1955. Earlier she held positions in school, college, and public libraries. She has served as a consultant in various aspects of librarianship both in the United States and in the Far East. She has been president of the Association of American Library Schools, the Library Education Division of the American Library Association, and the California Library Association. Dean Boaz has been author and editor of numerous books and articles, with special interests in library education, book selection, continuing education, research methods, and administration.

HERBERT GOLDHOR

Herbert Goldhor has been Director of the Graduate School of Library Science, University of Illinois, since 1962. He was formerly Chief Librarian of the Evansville (Indiana) Public Library. He is co-author of *Practical Administration of Public Libraries*, and his fields of interest include research in librarianship and public library administration.

MARY FRANCES K. JOHNSON

Mary Frances K. Johnson is Associate Professor and Chairman of the Library Education/Instructional Media Program, School of Education, University of North Carolina at Greensboro. She previously held positions as a school librarian and supervisor, and as a consultant in various development programs, including directorship of the School Library Development Project of the American Library Association. She has also been editor of *School Libraries*. In addition to school librarianship, her fields of special interest are children's and young adults' literature and reading guidance and audiovisual materials.

161

F. WILFRID LANCASTER

F. Wilfrid Lancaster is Professor of Library Science and Director of the Program in Biomedical Librarianship at the Graduate School of Library Science, University of Illinois. He has held various positions in systems evaluation and information retrieval services in the United States and Great Britain, including that of Information Systems Specialist, National Library of Medicine. He is the author of *Information Retrieval Systems* and *Vocabulary Control for Information Retrieval*. Other interests are medical libraries and industrial libraries.

STANLEY McELDERRY

Stanley McElderry is Director of the University of Chicago Library. He was formerly College Librarian, San Fernando Valley State College (California) and Dean of the Graduate School of Library Science, University of Texas. His special interest is the administration of academic libraries.

LOYD RATHBUN

Loyd Rathbun is Library Officer, Lincoln Laboratory, Massachusetts Institute of Technology. He was formerly librarian of the Hughes Aircraft Company Communications Division Library, Los Angeles. He has served on the Board of Directors of the Special Libraries Association, and has been active on the Association's Personnel and Standards Committees. He is a past president of the Boston Chapter of SLA.

DOROTHY SINCLAIR

Dorothy Sinclair has been Associate Professor, School of Library Science, Case Western Reserve University, since 1965. She was formerly Principal Librarian Consultant at the California State Library and Coordinator of Adult Services, Enoch Pratt Free Library. She is author of *Administration of the Small Public Library*, and is a specialist in adult services, reference, and public library administration.

C. WALTER STONE

C. Walter Stone is president of J-MARC, Inc. He has been a professor of library science in the library schools of the University of Pittsburgh and the University of Illinois, and has served as a consultant on survey teams studying book activity and needs in several foreign countries. His special interest is the administration of communication and information services.

PHYLLIS J. VAN ORDEN

Phyllis Van Orden is Associate Professor, Graduate School of Library Service, Rutgers University. She has been an elementary school librarian, children's librarian, and instructional materials consultant. Her special interest is in instructional materials centers.

INDEX